Lady Carolyne Lederer-Ralston, her honorary title coming from her architect husband's philanthropic knighthood, began writing a weekly newspaper gourmet cooking column in the mid-1970s. The Board of Education saw the gourmet columns and asked her to teach an adult night-school course for a new school. Their kitchen wasn't ready, so Carolyne agreed to teach the classes in her private home. Carolyne, as a hobby, is a food writer and an original recipe developer; while she has two contiguous careers, one for fifteen years as a textbook copy-editor, indexer and dictionary developer, working with international linguists and lexicographers. Since 1980 as an extremely successful realtor, she opened her own boutique real estate company, working alone since 1991, and having a 24% market share in her trading area, all the while she continued to write newspaper gourmet cooking columns.

To Sir James, with love—Boas to my Ruth.

Lady Carolyne Lederer-Ralston

FROM LADY RALSTON'S KITCHEN

Canadian Contessa Cooks—Gourmet in Every Bite

AUSTIN MACAULEY PUBLISHERS®

LONDON * CAMBRIDGE * NEW YORK * SHARJAH

Ordering Information
Quantity sales: Special discounts are available on quantity purchases by corporations, associations, and others. For details, contact the publisher at the address below.

Publisher's Cataloging-in-Publication data
Lederer-Ralston, Lady Carolyne.
From Lady Ralston's Kitchen

9781645361763 (Paperback)
9781645361756 (Hardback)
9781645366034 (ePub e-book)

Library of Congress Control Number: 2025908620

www.austinmacauley.com/us

First Published 2025
Austin Macauley Publishers LLC
40 Wall Street,33rd Floor, Suite 3302
New York, NY 10005
USA

mailto:mail-usa@austinmacauley.com
+1 (646) 5125767

Table of Contents

Foreword

The compilation of more than twelve hundred original recipes represents Lady Ralston's time in the kitchen for more than fifty years. When she was a child, she was never allowed in the spotless kitchen at home.

When she was in middle school, each student had to spend a few hours in homemaking classes each week: Cooking, cleaning, sewing, and learning how to follow patterns, recipes (and write them from memory), and preparation for eventually running a home; not unlike the characters in the reprinted title: "Perfection Salad" pedantic academic text.

When Lady Ralston was only twelve years old, there were three kitchens in the classroom environment; one had a gas range, the other two had electric ranges. The kitchens had stainless-steel sinks, and learning to clean them properly was part of the curriculum. If there was found one tiny water mark, the student assigned had to start all over again and rub and polish till the sinks looked brand new. Following World War II, stainless steel kitchen sinks were a new thing.

So, students learned to do things right the first time around, perhaps topics that were never addressed at home; whether "canning" peaches or tomatoes, baking puddings or bread. Due to scholastic budgets, the only meat worked with was ground beef, which, the following day, was served in the school cafeteria with (perfectly) mashed potatoes and a vegetable side.

And, oh yes: True; garbage was gift-wrapped, butcher shop style, in sheets of very clean, especially stored, newspaper, tied with string and deposited in immaculate covered trash cans. Never a mouse, a fly, or a visitor of any such acclaim; not ever. So Carolyne brought those learnings, along with her childhood spotless home requirements, later to her own home.

The teachers were old-fashioned British, strict, and literally force-fed the students to reach a goal of perfection. Never get a splatter on a cookbook. Put things back where you found them. Always.

Stand tall, don't slouch in the kitchen or at the sewing machine. Fingernails perfect and spotless, of course. Never bend the corner of a page in any book, and certainly don't ever break a book's or magazine's spine. Be sure glasses or cups were never touched with hands on their rims. When to use boiling water, hot water, cold water and for what. How to keep knives and scissors sharp and stored properly. The list is endless.

But it instilled a mindset in the students. Some left class no smarter than when they arrived. They simply weren't interested and that was reflected in their later life. It was the early 1950s and World War II had only been over a few years, and frugality was religiously practiced. Careful how much skin you take off the potato. And scrape carrots skin off with a sharp knife rather than peel the skins, and flush the carrot skins down the kitchen sewer drain to help keep it stable and from getting plugged. Carolyne still prepares carrots that way.

Others became deft at all the variables being taught in such a strict fashion. Things the author learned more than sixty years ago still apply in the running of her home and often are imbedded in her original recipes.

She grew up thinking everyone did what she did, the way she did it. As an adult she discovered that simply wasn't the way most people functioned. She was initially surprised.

So, as she compiled her gourmet newspaper columns from the 1970s, when gourmet locally was a whole new concept, weaving the recipes into what they are today, with amendments to reflect today's eating, she discovered she didn't just have recipes; she had stories imbedded.

***

Knowing, personally, the busy life of a working REALTOR® for nearly four decades after my children no longer lived at home, I can speak to a certain certainty as to how important it is to be organized if you plan to eat regularly, with or without children to feed. It's simply not sustainable, financially or health-wise, to live on drive-through edibles and totally rely on prepackaged foodstuffs. The body really does need "fresh," freshly prepared.

My recipes were all written with working people in mind because long before I became a REALTOR®, I already worked 60–80-hour weeks. But I was fortunate to maintain my full-time career, working from home. So, I had learned to multi-task long before the term was coined in the computer world. And I have included a segment at the end, called Timer, Timer, Timer, that readers are likely to find useful.

***

Knowing from personal experience, the often long hours that real estate professionals put in, I believe in cooking from scratch at every opportunity, so when I get home at odd hours or have to leave early in the morning to attend a class or a board or office meeting, there is always (my own) fast food available; ready to eat before I leave, or to take along with me, or to have at the ready when I return, ready to indulge with little effort.

I insist on only the best, fresh ingredients, and believe in shopping the sales and designing and creating my own recipes, mixing and matching odd foodstuffs at times. It is easy to sometimes make wonderful recipes from next to nothing; for example, I make a wickedly good ice cream using brandy marinated figs and homemade plum conserve. You will love my butter sautéed garlic shrimp in cognac cream sauce.

My Christmas goodies are always finished by the end of August, with the fruitcake marinating in brandy from then until the holiday season, so as to miss the Christmas rush.

Here, since the fresh fruit season will soon be with us, I'm starting off with this delightful old recipe from my writings in the 1970s.

Pavlova

History has it that the dessert Pavlova was first made with passion fruit about the turn of the century, in Australia, and was served to Anna Pavlova, a Russian ballerina.

You really must see this masterpiece to be able to appreciate its beauty. Give it a try. The only caveat is: Don't try to make Pavlova during humid weather. It won't dry properly and you will find it becomes a sticky, gooey mess, like melted marshmallow.

Will you believe you can prepare this dish yourself in less than 10 minutes? The only catch here (there had to be one) is that it takes two hours in the oven, but at only 250–275 F.

A busy Realtor has to eat, and often even finds time to entertain friends. You can make your Pavlova ahead because, stored in an airtight container, it will keep for up to six months, so this dish is ideal to keep on hand.

Make it early one morning or late one night, if you don't want your oven on during the heat of the day in summer weather. Or, toss it in the oven after you have had the oven on for some other dish. Just turn down the temperature, bake for one hour, turn off the oven and let the Pavlova sit undisturbed for another hour.

Pavlova has a reputation of being difficult to make. I've never been able to figure out why, but I think those comments come because it looks so impressive—and perhaps people fail to consider the weather. You can even take your ready-made Pavlova with you and assemble it at someone else's house, if you are requested to bring dessert.

This recipe will keep for a few days, even after filling, in the fridge. Slice and serve generous pieces in pie-shaped servings. It lifts easily with a cake knife.

Served in a swish French restaurant under the guise of Vacherin (whatever's; the names vary), with individually baked rings piled one on top of the other to form a very high case, filled with softened ice cream and then artfully decorated with fluffy whipped cream, it certainly is impressive and definitely does take more time and flair. But you will find this Bird's Nest Pavlova will create such a stir with your friends, they will have you labeled gourmet expert in no time.

Recipes for Pavlova come in many variations. Some use salad oil, salt, berry sugar and cream of tartar; others, vinegar; and still others, lemon and corn starch. My recipe is really a combination of other recipes that I have created to personalize it, and I prefer it to most others I have tried.

Bird's Nest Pavlova

6 or 8 egg whites (it really doesn't matter)

1–1¾ cup sugar (very fine, if available) (depending on how sweet your sweet tooth is)

1 tablespoon lemon juice

1 tablespoon cornstarch

Beat egg whites until stiff, but not dry, so you could turn the bowl over your head (don't try it when you've just come home from the hairdresser) and the egg whites won't move.

Add lemon and then the sugar gradually and sprinkle the cornstarch over and blend.

Put mixture onto a well-buttered and floured cookie sheet (use lightly oiled brown paper if you prefer, or parchment paper). With the back of a spoon, make a nest with high sides.

Flick the spoon for effect on the sides. Keep piling mixture up on the sides, smoothing the bottom a little. Ideally, keep mixture within a 10-inch circle.

Preheat oven to 350 F but as soon as you put the Pavlova into the oven, turn down the temperature control to 250–275 F.

Pavlova should be a warm, cream color, just off-white, not amber. The object is to dry the mixture, not to overcook it. After one hour, turn off the oven. Do not peek. Keep the door closed. Do not bake your Pavlova with the oven light on. Keeping an oven light on can sometimes alter the oven temperature if your thermostat is overly sensitive.

Let the Pavlova sit in the turned off oven for another hour or until cooled. Remove paper if used, and store in an airtight container.

Fill with stiff whipped cream and top with fresh fruit of your choice. For a different spin on the filling, try stirring hot chocolate dark powder into the whipped cream, or a little extra strong brewed coffee. *YUM!* Maybe use both and create mocha.

Brunch on the Run

1 chicken breast (cooked)
6 large mushrooms; chopped
2 egg whites
½ cup homemade mayonnaise
¾ cup mixed shredded cheeses (cheddar, parmesan and Romano)
1 green onion; chopped
Salt, pepper, thyme, vinegar

Cut cooked chicken into small chunks (use leftover chicken, if you have any)

Beat egg whites until stiff but not dry, add a few drops of vinegar. Sauté mushrooms. Stir mayonnaise into egg whites.

Add chicken pieces, mushrooms, mixed cheeses, green onion, salt pepper and thyme. Stir.

Butter eight slices of Vienna Crusty Bread, or something similar. Put a large spoonful of the mixture on each of four slices of bread.

Top with remaining four slices and put more chicken mixture on top. Sprinkle top with a little extra Romano cheese, and/or Parmesan; place on cookie sheet under broiler until bubbly and slightly brown on top.

This is economical, nutritious, and delicious! Serve straight from the oven or at room temperature; or cut into bite size pieces and plate so folks can help themselves. Great party dish, too. You will be making this a regular on your menu.

And, this is a great use for leftovers. Nothing gets wasted. When you are cooking, there is always another recipe in the making; just think it through. Ask yourself: What can I do with this, rather than toss it in the trash? Even a leftover barbecued piece of chicken will work here, but the taste will be very different. It is a great way to get teens to pop some real food into their mouths on the way out the door. But whatever you do, don't tell them it's good for them.

Caution: The scent created while the cheeses are melting may attract your neighbors.

Holiday Magic—No Matter
What You Celebrate

The holiday entertaining season presents an opportunity for us to try new and different recipes. Your guests will long remember these ones: ENJOY!

Asbach Cheese Ball

254 g cream cheese

120 g Canadian medium cheddar cheese; grated

70 g blue cheese

1 clove garlic; minced and crushed

1 g chopped fresh chives (soak dry chives in the Asbach)

15 ml Asbach Uralt brandy 45 ml sour cream

Cream the cream cheese at room temperature for about five minutes, using the dough hook of your kitchen machine. Still using the dough hook, add the other ingredients and combine well. Heap the mixture onto a piece of cello wrap and wrap well. Store for an hour or so in the refrigerator or until the consistency is such that you can work with it. Form a large ball and roll in crushed walnuts. Chill or freeze until party day. Serve at room temperature.

Variations: Make 1 ½-inch balls from the cheese mixture and roll them in walnuts.

Asbach Cheese Dip: Add a little more sour cream to the above recipe (about half a small dish) and stir well. It's a super dip to serve with chips or crackers, but especially good with homemade croissants.

Canadian Cheddar Cheese Balls

1 cup Canadian cheddar cheese; grated

1 tablespoon parmesan cheese; grated

1 tablespoon Romano cheese; grated

1 egg; separated

¼ cup seasoned coarse fresh breadcrumbs

¼ teaspoon French's prepared mustard (or Dijon for a completely different taste)

Salt to taste

Pinch cayenne pepper

For rolling—very fine seasoned breadcrumbs

Mix all of the ingredients together except the egg white. Whip the egg white until very stiff but not dry and fold into cheese mixture. Form into bite-size balls and roll in very fine seasoned breadcrumbs. Deep fry a small quantity at a time for just a few seconds.

Regular seasoned breadcrumbs are made by adding your favorite herbs and spices. I use 1 teaspoon thyme, ½ teaspoon poultry seasoning, salt and pepper to 2 cups of breadcrumbs.

Variation: Roll cheese balls in ground walnuts instead of fine crumbs. Perhaps try Panko crumbs. Delicious!

Bitterballen (Veal Croquettes)

Traditionally served at New Year's or Christmas, these delightful meatballs will have all your guests coming back for seconds and thirds. They are good year-round, not just for special occasions.

The bitterballen are deep-fried and served piping hot with hot mustard; keep them warm in the oven until serving time or make them ahead and reheat in 300 F oven for about half an hour prior to serving. The name is misleading, because there is nothing bitter about them. The name comes from the occasions on which they are served, when "bitters" are frequently offered along with drinks, particularly gin. This is traditionally a Dutch treat, but the following is my own creation and we serve it all year round to family and friends who drop in.

Bitterballen freeze well, so you can always have some on hand. They will keep for several days in the coldest part of the fridge, although they will not keep indefinitely because of the cream content. So, you really do not think much of veal? Kind of blah and tasteless, you say? Your husband wouldn't eat veal, so no sense even trying this recipe? Well, if you insist. Funny, I am sure he would be back for seconds at my house.

1 pound ground veal
¼ pound ground pork
Salt, pepper, Italian seasoning
Garlic salt
Thyme
Sage
1 egg, beaten
¾ cup course breadcrumbs, brown or cracked wheat
Chopped parsley
2 tablespoon cream
Seasoned breadcrumbs
Beaten eggs
Oil or lard for deep-frying

Mix all ingredients in large mixing bowl and form 1-inch balls (rather large). Cover with oiled waxed paper if you aren't going to deep-fry them straight away. Roll balls in beaten egg and then in seasoned breadcrumbs. Deep-fry. Test oil with cube of dry bread. Bread should deep-fry to a beautiful golden color on both sides in about 60 seconds; or with thermometer, oil should reach 375 F, not hotter or it will smoke. I always deep-fry using corn oil.

You should always use a deep cast-iron pot or a heavy baked-enamel pot for deep-frying, if you don't have a deep-fryer. Never try to deep-fry in an aluminum pot and do not have liquid fat deeper than half way up the side of the pot. Bitterballen will cook in about 3–4 minutes on each side. Makes about 30. (Plan on 4–6 per person because they'll be back for seconds.)

Instant Fresh Tomato Basil Salad

Here's one you can't mess up. Cut up a yummy (seeded) large, fresh, red tomato into small pieces. Mince (chop very fine) about a teaspoon of fresh white onion. Put both in a small mixing bowl. If you like a bit of garlic, mince a very tiny piece. Add a little salt and fresh ground pepper and a generous pinch of dried thyme, but not the kind that looks like ground pepper. Make sure it's just a pinch because it's powerful.

Open a tin of chickpeas (garbanzo beans), drain them and rinse off the starch.

Add about a quarter of the peas to the tomato bowl (save the rest in a covered container in the fridge…they keep). Now add a couple of tablespoons of your favorite olive oil, a little white Balsamic vinegar (just a spritz—and this recipe works best only with "white" Balsamic—Fortino's is the best one I have found to date)…and adjust salt to your taste. Toss with a tiny squirt of fresh squeezed lemon juice. Add just a little sprinkle of dried ground Parmesan.

Buy a little jar of artichoke hearts in olive oil. Keep the opened jar in the fridge—it lasts a long time. Take a couple of the artichoke hearts from the oil, and chop loosely and place on side of each salad plate just before serving. Add a teaspoon of the artichoke oil, and a tiny bit of the minced artichokes floating in the oil, to the tomato dish. If you like to cook with spirits, add a tiny splash of your favorite brandy.

Just before serving, finely chop about a half-teaspoon of fresh basil leaves and sprinkle on the salad. Give a quick toss and serve over shredded (horizontally) romaine lettuce leaves, or place on top of Boston Leaf Lettuce. Ideally use the hydroponically grown Boston Bibb lettuce. It really does taste different, and I think, better. Always wash lettuce well, under quite hot running water (yes, you read that right—quite hot water). Shake the lettuce and pat dry. Roll the lettuce up securely in a clean light-weight kitchen towel and store in the fridge in a plastic bag until you are ready to use it. This works really well for romaine lettuce also. The lettuce will be crisp as though you had just picked it from the garden.

Prep time: Less than five minutes. Amazingly simple, and DELICIOUS! Try it. You will love it. It can be made ahead of time, except for adding the fresh basil. Add the basil just before eating. I serve this salad with Havarti sun-dried tomato cheese and Melba toast on a side plate. This salad looks particularly nice served on a black plate.

I love it, and salad doesn't get better than this. It's fresh and delicious and your friends and colleagues will beg for more. Remember, first we eat with our eyes. Serves two.

This salad makes a great Sunday morning brunch, served as a first course, followed by seared chicken livers, mushrooms and onions and a sprinkle of dried thyme. Salt and pepper it when cooked. Keep the liver mix warm in a chafing dish, served alongside a great cream of roasted multi-colored bell pepper soup, and your favorite fresh baked bread.

Getting Ahead of the Holiday Season

Asbach Uralt is the brandy of brandies, but in Ontario the LCBO had been delisted but is now available once again. Although it is unique, and the only one I have used for more than 30 years, try your own favorite brandy and I am sure you will still enjoy the results.

Stollen is as old as history itself, and it is said to have originally been made as a symbol of the Christ child wrapped in swaddling clothes. Stollen can be made as bare or as elaborate as the budget permits, having only raisins in during lean years and being plumped up with fruits of all description in the fat years. But don't skimp on the brandy, for its subtle flavor enhances the actual flavor of this country-German fare in an incomparable fashion.

This recipe is produced entirely in metric. Every kitchen should have a small scale.

I played with some of my yeast doughs as I tested them over the years, and decided on one to turn into Stollen, my way. There's a multitude of variations, as different provinces create their own versions all over Europe.

If you do not have a heavy-duty mixer, old-fashioned (strong) wooden spoons, bowls and hands will certainly suffice; you will just have a little more work to produce the finished product. If you are a bread maker anyhow, you will understand, and will appreciate the exquisite texture of this dough. If you own another machine, adapt the directions to those accompanying your equipment.

Asbach Stollen

1 cup candied mixed peel

1 cup mixed red and green candied cherries, cut in half

55 ml Asbach Uralt Brandy (or your favorite brandy)

½ cup fresh, slivered almonds; unblanched

¼ cup freshly shelled and chopped walnuts (really the shelled ones have a different taste)

Soak fruit in 55 ml brandy for 2–3 hours prior to making recipe. Sliver nuts with food slicer attachment of your kitchen machine or with a very sharp knife (cautiously)

1 (8g) pkg dry yeast

200 ml warm milk

3 g sugar

350 g flour

80 g sugar

60 g softened unsalted butter

1 warmed egg, beaten (let egg come to room temperature, then stand it in a cup of warm, not hot, water for a few minutes). Always cook or bake with eggs at room temperature for best results (even when you are doing hard cooked eggs).

Measure 200 ml milk into a beaker. Heat this milk but do not boil. In a warm dish, place 3 g sugar and 100 ml of the milk (reserve the rest). Stir well to dissolve sugar. Add dry yeast and give a little stir. Set timer for 15 minutes. When timer rings, stir yeast mixture well. It will have puffed up in the dish and will deflate when you stir.

In the meantime, place flour, sugar, softened unsalted butter and the remaining warm milk into the large bowl of the kitchen mixing machine (not a food processor), along with the beaten egg.

Add yeast mixture and set machine in operation, using the dough hook. Mix for about five minutes on low/slow speed.

This mixing process actually kneads the batter for you, so at this point, batter will have left the sides of the bowl and will be a turning blob on the dough hook. Dough will be very pliable and somewhat shiny looking.

Place dough in a warm glass or baked enamel bowl and cover with a clean towel. Allow to double in size in a warm, draft-free place. (About 1–1½ hours.).

Dredge fruit and nuts in a few grams of flour (just enough so fruit doesn't stick together). Sprinkle fruit with a couple of grams of salt and a few drops of natural real almond flavoring (do not use artificial flavorings). A friend brought me a terrific brand of vanilla and almond flavoring from her trip to Aruba, and I kept it for really special recipes like this one.

Knead fruit mixture into punched down dough, adding only a small amount at a time. Knead for several minutes, but don't handle the dough unnecessarily. Don't force dough; knead it gently.

With a rolling pin, gently roll dough on very lightly floured board, into a large oval shape about 1 cm thick. Fold dough off-center lengthwise, plumping it up a bit near the center. This creates a ridge down the off-center midpoint. Brush with a little unsalted butter and place on a well-buttered cookie sheet. Cover and put in a warm place to double in bulk.

Bake at 400 F for about 40 minutes. Remove and place on rack to cool. Brush with butter again while still warm. After Asbach Stollen is (absolutely) completely cool, sprinkle with icing sugar, sifted over top. Store in a sealed air-tight plastic bag. Store for a few weeks in a cool place. All the flavors meld during the wait-time and create a whole new scent that is irresistible. Serve, sliced, with all your other Christmas goodies. The scent of the brandied fruit will stay with you as a reminder to make this a seasonal favorite.

Served with a plate of mixed cheeses, a few green grapes and perhaps accompanying your favorite wines or sherry, your guest table will be the talk of the town.

Instant Rose Pasta Sauce (And Several Additional Uses)

In a wide low skillet, on high heat, scald two cups of half-and-half cream. You cannot turn your back on the skillet, even for a second. The cream needs to rise to the top. Lift the skillet quickly as cream approaches the top of pan so that it does not over boil, because it makes a very big nasty mess on your stovetop if that happens.

Turn down the heat so that the cream continues to cook but not burn. The cream will thicken considerably. Stir it a few times, wiping down the edges of the pan with your wooden spoon or a rubber spatula. Salt and add fresh ground pepper, a pinch of dry thyme and a pinch of garlic salt.

Stir in a third to a half cup of your favorite two cheeses; grated. I prefer Romano and Parmesan mixed for this recipe. You can use dried ready-grated cheese.

In a tall but narrow pot or bowl, cover one large fresh red tomato with boiling water. Let it sit briefly, then dunk the tomato into a pot of ice water. The skin will slip right off. Remove seeds, core and chop coarsely. Add to the cream mixture in the skillet. Add minced fresh green basil leaves (about a quarter cup). I don't like purple grape color basil in this recipe.

Stir in egg noodle pasta that has been cooked, al dente, in boiling salted water, drained and tossed with a little real butter (this recipe really does need that butter) and a drop of your favorite olive oil (stops pasta from sticking together). Serve.

Prep time 20 minutes. This sauce is even more fabulous the second day. Reheat gently with fresh cooked pasta in the sauce. The sauce can be made a day ahead, reheated and served over fresh cooked very hot pasta.

Other Suggestions

Serve over rotini pasta. This curled pasta keeps the sauce in the grooves of the pasta nicely. Before serving, try adding fresh cooked shrimp and/or large whole sea scallops that are just barely cooked (about three minutes each side, in real butter of course, with a pinch of thyme).

Fresh poached lobster is fabulous with this sauce. Add sliced mushrooms that have been cooked: Once over easy in sizzling real butter. You could mince a tablespoon of onion and add it if you like. Another alternative: Fry three slices of bacon until quite crispy. Break bacon into quarter-inch pieces so you can see them in the mix. Add just before serving.

One More Choice

Poach fresh lobster pieces in an abundance of real butter (save the leftover butter to cook shrimp or scallops in); add a little tiny bit of dry thyme and salt, or use large pieces of tinned, frozen lobster tossed in a bit of sizzling butter just to warm; add lobster to the sauce right at the end, just before serving. You don't want to continue cooking the lobster.

Alternate serving instead of with pasta: Serve in a rolled, freshly made thin crepe. Place the filled crepe in a hot, buttered, but not burning hot skillet and flambé with your favorite brandy or bitters. Decorate each of the plates with a sprig of fresh, brilliant green basil, just plucked from the pot.

For an extra decorative serving idea, add a dollop of whipped cream (add just a little sugar and a tiny drizzle of vanilla, the way you would for a dessert cream) into which you have stirred a tablespoon of finely minced (fresh only) basil leaves. Stick a basil leaf into the dollop so people will know what is in it. Whipped cream will turn a little green and people will wonder what is in it, but with the basil trimming, they might guess. These uses of the rose [French accent] sauce are so YUM!

A Mommessin Beaujolais or a Chianti is nice with this dish.

Sacrilegious Shiraz-Permeated Veal Shoulder (Or Shank)

About a pound of veal shoulder, bone in. Looks like a large steak. Let meat come to room temperature before browning, but don't leave it out for too long.

Three medium carrots
½ cup leek slices from the mid-section of the leek
Two medium-large onions
Several whole garlic cloves (they will disappear in cooking, and cooked this way you won't even taste the garlic; just enhances flavor)
Salt, pepper, a pinch of dried thyme
2/3 to 1 cup of homemade tomato sauce (like you use for spaghetti) made from tomato paste. (Always keep some in the fridge—made from onion, fresh only garlic, thyme and tomato paste and a little chicken broth. (It keeps for a long time in a glass covered stainless steel container)
¼ cup butter
4 tablespoons Mazola Corn oil

Shiraz red wine (ideal is Obikwa from South Africa)—Full bodied, almost dry, this wine keeps in the fridge, tightly covered, for a very long time. Never toss out leftover part bottles of wine. Save for cooking

Slightly brown the butter and oil on high heat (just golden not dark brown). Be careful not to burn. Lay the flat meat into a heavy very hot stew pot. Salt and pepper the meat. Brown both sides quickly and turn down the heat right away or the meat will get tough. (If you miss and this happens, don't dispose of the meat; use it to make a pate—a recipe for another day). Stay with the pot during browning. Quite dark brown.

While the second side is browning, lay the garlic (whole) pieces on top of the meat. Leave the garlic in that position permanently. Turn down the heat to medium, and cover for about 10–15 minutes. Turn the meat only once more, near the end of cooking.

Wash carrots and chop into bite size pieces. Split onions in half and remove skin. Split in half lengthwise again. Slice the leek into thin coins and wash well in a sieve or strainer to make sure all the sand is out. Add the vegetables to the pot. Add a little salt.

Let simmer, covered, on medium high heat for about 10 more minutes. Watch carefully. Add the tomato sauce. Cover and leave on very low heat, lowest setting for one hour, checking occasionally to make sure it is not burning. Sticking to the bottom of the pot is okay. Resist the urge to stir too much.

Then pull the meat off the bones using two forks. Boil the bones in a half cup of cold water for a few minutes and strain the broth into the meat pot. Leave the meat in the pot. By now the texture should be like a goulash. The carrots still whole, but the onions and leeks will have almost disappeared. Stir, scrape the bottom of the pot. Cover and return to heat for at least a half hour. Taste to adjust salt.

Pour into the meat pot, about 2/3 cup of Shiraz. Stir once. Cover. Return to lowest heat setting for about 10–15 minutes. Watch carefully. Remove lid and stir once. Cover. Turn off heat. Let sit until you can test without burning your mouth. Yummmm! Pour into a glass (only) container and cover the container with plastic wrap and place the lid on the dish. Let it sit on the counter for a half-hour or so (not in summer weather), and then store overnight in the fridge. You can serve this dish right away; it just gets better later. Will keep for several days. Remove from the fridge at least an hour before serving time. Reheat gently (not in microwave) in a heavy bottom saucepan on very low heat. Watch carefully so it does not stick and burn. The Shiraz is not terribly sweet, but adds just the right amount of palette teasing sweetness to the dish. AMAZING flavor!

Serve with spaetzle (pasta), egg noodles, rice or creamy whipped potatoes. Or maybe alongside my French Faux Aligot recipe. Looks like goulash. Carrots and green beans make best side serve dishes.

If you wish, stir in a half cup of sour cream just before serving (do not reheat after the sour cream is added; it might separate). Not necessary at all, but just a different version to turn this into a party dinner. Enjoy!

Ever Try Chicken Livers?

If not, you will enjoy this recipe.

Want a special but down-to-earth brunch for the coming weekend? Filling and satisfying food, but not heavy and hard to digest? Then try this wonderful recipe that is special all year 'round. After a late sleep in on a Sunday morning, this makes an ideal tummy healer that sits well as it digests.

This recipe is best when it is served fresh, hot from the pan, or even at room temperature, but it will keep a day in the fridge.

Check this out: If you have never eaten chicken livers, don't be put off by how they look, or how they feel. Have paper towel handy, a clean soapy dishcloth and drying towel. This, after all, is chicken, and you don't want to handle chicken at any time without washing your hands, the counters and utensils. Handle your taps with the paper towel, so you never transfer salmonella. It can make you very sick. Cooking kills it, but the raw effects need to be avoided.

The King's Breakfast or Brunch

¾ pound fresh chicken livers—not frozen (buy them a day or two before using, ideally)
¼ of a large Spanish onion; chopped coarsely but a little fine
10 or 12 large button mushrooms; stems removed and chopped separately
Salt, pepper, dry thyme (not the kind that looks like pepper)
Unsalted butter
2 Tablespoons Winzertanz (white wine)

Rinse the chicken livers. I use a small colander; drain and pat dry with paper towel. Remove any yellow or green bits of gall with a sharp knife; you will want to leave the chicken livers whole.

In a hot skillet, sauté chopped onion in butter, stirring until onion is translucent. Turn down heat as necessary to prevent burning. Don't be stingy with the butter, and cook until just barely a golden color and onions are fully cooked, but not mushy.

Add to onions the mushrooms that you have cut into chunks or quarters and sautéed for only a couple of minutes on high heat; you want the mushrooms just once over lightly. (Martha Stewart cooks mushrooms far too long!) The moisture from the onions and butter should keep the onions from sticking to the pan, but add a little more butter as necessary because you must keep the pan as hot as possible without burning.

Rest this lot in a heatproof bowl. Turn unwashed used skillet onto very high heat and add the chopped chicken livers when butter begins to sizzle, but not burn. You want to scorch the surface of the livers. Don't touch them for a few seconds. They will appear to stick to the pan, but this is all right.

Reduce heat ever so slightly, add salt and pepper, and dry thyme—just a pinch because dry thyme delivers a very powerful punch; you want the flavor to enhance the dish, not take it over. Turn the chicken livers, one by one, individually. They should still be pink inside. They are cooked at this stage. Do not overcook them. The livers should be moist and juicy. Add the chicken livers to the onions and mushrooms and stir. Keep hot. Although you might want to cover them, keep any cover at a slight tilt; you don't want to steam them. They will continue to cook in their own heat.

Deglaze the skillet with Winzertanz (the flavor of the ingredients in this particular wine enhance the flavor of the dish), scraping and saving any stuck-on bits, and pour over the mixture in the dish. Serve, piping hot with fresh toast (try cutting off the crusts if you are using buttered white bread toast), or use fresh rye bread, untoasted. Again, perhaps cut off the crusts or even use a large cookie cutter and make bread "rounds."

All of this preparation has taken less than 15 minutes. It is also great for a midnight snack. If guests are staying over, this brunch will make a delightful surprise for them.

Can be used as a *hors dourest* if you chop the livers finely, after they are cooked. If you really want to have some fancy *hors d'oeuvre*, process the whole recipe after it is cooked, until it forms a spreadable pate. Top with a piece of raw mushroom. Or using larger button mushrooms with stems removed, use the pate to stuff mushrooms. Top with a sprig of fresh thyme. So YUM!

Delicious Dips for Crudités

Crudités are very popular all year round—as *hors oeuvres* or just as everyday snacks. The name comes from the word *crude*, which means in its raw or natural state. Save this recipe for the summer, when all the Canadian grown vegetables are so plentiful—that's the time to make large plates full of carrot strips, celery sticks, broccoli and cauliflower flowerets, green onions, green, red, yellow and orange peppers and cherry tomatoes in all colors. The sky's the limit. Any or all of these vegetables can be presented in a most appetizing way on kitchen dishes, fine dinner china, or even on paper plates.

With summer being such a short season in this country, you'll want to take advantage of your garden goodies as often as possible and there's no better way to acquire all your body's food requirements than to munch on raw vegetables. Keep a bowl of prepared dip on hand and along with those barbecued steaks, chicken or fish, you'll have a full-course, nutrition-packed meal. Here are a few recipes for favorite dips.

¾ pound creamy cottage cheese

2 green onions, chopped fine

Salt, pepper and a sprinkle of parsley

Combine all ingredients well. Chill. Serve with fresh vegetables.

OR

½ pound cream cheese (Philadelphia)

¼ teaspoon ground oregano

¼ teaspoon Italian seasoning

¼ teaspoon loose dry thyme

Sprinkle paprika

Sprinkle garlic salt

1½ teaspoon vermouth

Drop of Tabasco sauce

Combine all ingredients well. Chill. Serve with fresh vegetables.

OR

1 small carton of sour cream

3 teaspoon finely chopped chives (or substitute chopped dill)

salt and pepper

Combine all ingredients well. Chill. Serve with fresh vegetables.

You can mix and match any of these variations. Try it. You'll come back for more.

Spectacular Indoor-Outdoor Desserts

These heavy cream recipes are not for the faint of heart but because they are made at home and have no preservatives, at least you know what you are eating. A little goes a very long way. Keep refrigerated until serving.

They are beautiful, served in crystal goblets at a formal occasion or special served in a see-through plastic goblet outside on the patio after a wonderful barbecue. Sounds like a heavy dessert, but you will find these recipes light and they go down well after a big meal. Guests will think you have put in a lot of effort to please their taste buds.

Most people who entertain on a regular basis will find that keeping these ingredients on hand will enable them to become instant gourmets when unexpected guests appear. Or, after a busy day at work or on the road, these concoctions can be whipped up in a big hurry (pardon the pun), prior to making your family meal. They can rest in the fridge while you eat your dinner, indoors or out.

Banana Flambé with Chantilly Cream

Bananas are an excellent source of nutrition. Include them regularly in your diet and in school lunches. Although the price for bananas keeps creeping up, if you watch the store specials, you will find them at respectable prices from time to time. For this recipe, you need firm, solid but ripe bananas. Don't use mushy ones.

Nearly everyone has a favorite receipt for banana bread or can toss together an age-old favorite, the banana split.

This recipe has been a favorite around our house for years and years. Recently I saw a version of this recipe billed as coming from a swank New Orleans' restaurant. I did not know whether to laugh or cry. Here I had been thinking myself terribly clever all these years, making up this recipe in less than five minutes—for more than 40 years.

Melt a quarter cup of unsalted butter and stir in a ½ cup of brown sugar. Do not let this stay on the fire too long, just until blended. Sauté three bananas, quartered, in the hot butter and brown sugar for about three minutes.

Sprinkle a little cardamom over the bananas and flambé with two ounces of Southern Comfort. Serve over very cold firm Chantilly cream in individual serving dishes.

Hot sauce will cause the edges of the thick cream (almost like ice cream) to go a little soupy, but that's what's supposed to happen. Aren't you drooling already?

To make the Chantilly cream, use two 10oz. containers of heavy cream, whipped; two-thirds cup of white sugar; and a half-teaspoon of vanilla.

Crème Chantilly Ananas

2–10 oz containers of heavy (35%) cream
2/3 cup fine white sugar (not confectioners)
1 teaspoon vanilla
1–19 oz-20oz tin "crushed" Dole pineapple; drained (ideally buy the one in sugar syrup although it is very hard to find now). You might have to make your own sugar syrup.

Whip the two containers of heavy cream until quite stiff, but still fluffy. Slowly add the sugar, mixing on the slow speed of the mixer, so as only to incorporate the sugar and not turn the cream into butter. Stir in vanilla. Refrigerate in the coldest part of fridge (near the back usually) until serving time.

When ready to serve, fold strained/drained pineapple into the mixture and transfer to a large crystal or glass serving bowl. (So that guests can see the cream). Serve dessert at the table in open wide-surface old-fashioned champagne glasses at a formal meal, or outside at the patio in plastic serving dishes after a backyard barbecue. This dessert is fluffy and light and very impressive; having been chilled, it has the consistency of ice cream.

Serve Crème Chantilly Ananas after a heavy meal, when you do not wish to. If you like, top the bowl with candied pineapple as a garniture or use a few soft centered chocolates. Serves eight.

Delicious Tortillas for Lunch

This is great finger food for party time or ball game treats —warm, soft, extra-large tortillas; sun-dried tomato basil; spinach or plain. For this recipe the tortillas will be used flat. Use two—one on top of the other like a big round sandwich.

Prepare chicken filling: Using leftover roast chicken pieces (you could use tinned tuna or any other filling that is your favorite), place meat into a strong blender or food processor. Whir until tiny chunks appear. Add small chunks of medium cheddar cheese, a small spoon of sour cream, a little mayonnaise, a small piece of garlic and a tiny piece of green onion and a pinch of thyme, and a little sprinkle of fresh ground pepper. Add a little grated sharp Parmesan cheese. If the mixture is too dry, add a tablespoon or two of chicken broth or leftover gravy. Process until nearly smooth. Place in covered container. It's better the next day, but perfectly fine to use immediately.

Prepare roast beef or leftover steak filling: Using leftover beef pieces (you could use pork or lamb or any other filling that is your favorite), place meat into strong blender or food processor. Whir until tiny chunks appear. Add small chunks of medium cheddar cheese, two or three pimento filled olives, a small spoon of sour cream, a little mayonnaise, a small piece of garlic and a tiny piece of regular onion and a pinch of thyme and a little sprinkle of fresh ground pepper. Add a little grated sharp Parmesan cheese. If mixture is too dry, add a tablespoon or two of chicken broth or leftover gravy or beef drippings. Process until nearly smooth. Place in covered container. It's better the next day, but perfectly fine to use immediately.

Spread filling on one of the warmed soft tortillas; sprinkle with a couple of finger-minced fresh basil leaves (more if you love it so much). Top with second warm tortilla. Cut in half width-wise. Cut in half again. Keep cutting in half by rotating until you have eight pieces. Cover with plastic wrap and use for tasty snacks after school or while you are on the run. Will keep for a couple of days in the refrigerator. A great grab and run food for Realtors and/or for lunch box treats for the kids. Don't tell them it's good for them. Once you make these, you will expect they should always be on hand. Made in minutes. So easy. Such a tasty use for leftovers.

Creative additions: Slice a tart-sweet apple; cover chicken filling with the apple slices, or just dot the service with a few slices. Add a few walnut pieces and cover the filling with soft Boston lettuce leaves. Spread cover tortilla with mayonnaise or your favorite sauce. Place on top. Cut same as before into pie-shaped pieces…now you have a Waldorf salad lunch or light dinner. So GOOD! Great warm or cold.

Meatless filling: At 425 F for about 25–30 minutes, roast chunks of eggplant, zucchini, onions, peppers, firm tomatoes (maybe even green tomatoes), whole cloves of garlic that have been tossed in your favorite olive oil, salt and cracked black pepper. I like to use half and half melted butter and corn oil. Sprinkle with dried thyme and/or dried basil (just a pinch), or a little Italian seasoning. If you like a Tex-Mex flavor, add some chilies to the mix. Let cool, then pulse till coarse consistency; add your favorite Feta cheese for a nice cheesy-veg spread. Spread on warm tortillas. Slice and serve warm or cold. Will keep for several days in refrigerator.

Seafood filling: Using tinned or cooked lobster, shrimp and scallops, add a pinch of garlic, a pinch of green onion, your favorite cheese (I know—people don't always want to use cheese with seafood), along with a little

Parmesan grated, a little sour cream and a little mayonnaise; whir in the food processor. If filling is too stiff, add a couple of tablespoons of cream. Use same day, ideally.

If using as an *hors d'oeuvres*, perhaps using a small decorative toothpick, top seafood slice with a full-size shrimp or a slice of scallop.

Topping for beef or other meat filling: Try a wedge or slice of hard-cooked egg, sprinkled with paprika.

Topping for chicken: Perhaps an olive, a cheddar curl or a tomato rose.

Topping for veggie filling: Try a whole black olive positioned strategically on a fancy toothpick; or use a cherry tomato or a roasted whole garlic bud. Garlic develops a sweet flavor when roasted whole. It's soft, spreadable and wonderful. Not nearly as potent as raw garlic.

Mix and match or serve on easily identifiable plates of all one kind. Have guests serve themselves. Better make plenty. They'll be back for more. There won't be leftovers.

Pesto

Made a little differently (a la watercress).

1 ½ tablespoon roasted hazelnuts
2 cups packed watercress leaves and tender stems
1 small, young green onion, loosely chopped with a knife
6 tablespoon extra-virgin olive oil
½ cup shredded parmesan cheese
Salt (optional)
8 oz. of your favorite pasta—or homemade spaetzle

Coarsely chop nuts in a food processor. Add watercress leaves, green onion, olive oil and cheese.

Pulse until as smooth or coarse purée as you prefer. Add just a sprinkle of salt.

Stir into cooked pasta. Garnish with a tomato rose. (Made by slicing a ripe tomato with a sharp serrated knife, running the knife round and round the tomato surface creating a long, wide string-like strip of tomato flesh. Position the strip in the shape of a flower to create a tomato rose.)

The tomato rose can be used as a garnish on many dishes. Try using a ripe yellow tomato for a fresh new take on the tomato rose. Position the rose on a tiny arrangement of fresh basil leaves, on the side of the serving dish. Voila…Instant gourmet.

Served in small side dishes, this is an ideal accompaniment to barbecued fish or alongside any other dish. Since it is so light and fresh, everyone will enjoy its wonderful texture and taste.

No Excuse not to Eat Spinach

Here is an easy summer recipe that I put together quite by accident recently and it was so delicious that I thought I should share it.

Gather as much special tender spinach (flat-leaf tender young leaves) as you require for a good plate-full of salad (washed and dried in a tea towel); one or two cold quartered boiled eggs (or as many as you like); a handful of very fresh, chopped or sliced, white button mushrooms; and sweet black olives, whole (as many as you like—they are absolutely delicious!).

On a serving plate or bowl, place equal parts of your favorite olive oil and top-of-the-line balsamic black vinegar. Add a pinch of dried basil and a pinch of dried mint and sprinkle with fresh ground peppercorns. Add a little sweet paprika powder to the chopped hard-boiled eggs. There is no salt in this recipe (unless you crave it). Garnish with large shrimp or tomato wedges.

That's it! Just add a portion of the spinach mixture, and you have as many individual servings as you need. Toss with two forks on your own plate (this way the leftover greens mixture can be placed in the fridge in a sealed plastic food bag for later in the day, or if you are lucky, for the next day's lunch). Enjoy!

Here's another spinach recipe you can enjoy any time of the year

Wash spinach well to remove sand particles. Shake off excess water, but do not dry the leaves. Place in a covered skillet, and "sweat" the spinach the way you would onions, until spinach is "just wilted". The excess water will be in the bottom of the pan. Drain spinach in a colander. Push out the excess water from the spinach and toss out any leftover water from the skillet.

In the same skillet, on medium high heat, cook finely chopped rashers of bacon until nearly crisp, but not crunchy. Remove bacon from pan and keep warm on a covered plate, leaving the stuck-on bits on the bottom of the pan. If there is a lot of excess fat, remove some of it, but not all. Leave perhaps three tablespoons of the bacon fat, for an average family-size serving of spinach.

In the same skillet, sauté a half-cup of finely chopped sweet white onions, until they are "just" done, not overcooked. When the onions are nearly cooked, add a smashed garlic clove, keeping the heat down. Careful not to burn the garlic or you won't be able to eat it. Toss gently and add a little salt and freshly ground pepper. Add the chopped, cooked bacon back into the skillet. Turn off the heat and set aside to keep warm for a few seconds while you finish the spinach.

After all the excess moisture has been pushed out of the spinach, place it on a cutting board and gently chop with a sharp knife. Add chopped spinach to bacon, onion and garlic mix. Place in a serving dish that you have warmed with boiling water, because spinach cools rapidly.

Now deglaze the skillet with your favorite brandy or cognac. The alcohol will vanish, just leaving the flavor. Just a few tablespoons will do it. Scrape the bits from the bottom of the pan using an egg turner backward and pour the spirits over the spinach mixture.

Serve with your favorite vegetables and meat for dinner.

This same mixture can be used for stuffing a rolled veal or pork roast, and can also be used to stuff an omelet or crepe for a nice light lunch or brunch. If you really want to go overboard, serve a dollop of sour crème with the omelet or crepe. YUMMMM! There won't be leftovers.

Mealtime Economy Special is Delicious

In home economics classes, they used to teach all sorts of "techniques"—of course for me, World War II had only been over a few years and most people were still very much "economy minded." We were taught how to extend food to make it stretch to feed more people, yet not have people question what exactly caused a small purchase to go so far. Sort of the loaves and fishes concept.

This dish can be served with glorious mashed whipped potatoes or rice, or split and used on an Italian bun, smothered in the peppers. This dish makes its own sauce in the baking process and the sauce can be used as gravy for the potatoes or drizzled over the meatballs in the sandwich. Either way, those who eat it won't soon forget how delicious it tasted.

It's little bit of a nuisance to prepare, but not at all difficult. It tastes spectacular as leftovers, cut in thick slices for a packed lunch sandwich on rye bread or regular bread. It's important to follow the directions about splitting the oversize meatballs and putting a generous sprinkle of grated cheese on—right at the time of serving, not sooner. Do it just as you plate the food—it makes all the difference.

Gourmet Meatballs ~ Extended

Makes 6 meatballs (1= cup-size). Split in half when serving and sprinkle 1 tablespoon grated Parmesan cheese on each half. Serve with "sweated" onion pieces, green and red and yellow sweet bell peppers cut in chunks and par-boiled for 3 minutes, then sautéed lightly and quickly in a mix of very hot—but not so hot as to burn—corn oil and real butter, before baking with the meatballs. Empty the sauté pan, sauce and all, over the meatballs before placing the pan in the oven.

Ingredients:

1¼ —1½ pounds of ground beef
8 slices day old white bread soaked in ½ cup milk
1 egg
1 teaspoon crushed thyme leaves
1½ teaspoon salt
½ teaspoon pepper
Parsley
1 tablespoon poultry seasoning
3 tablespoon grated Parmesan cheese
1½ tablespoon grated Romano cheese
5 olives stuffed (red pepper) chopped very fine
6 coarsely chopped mushrooms (quartered is good)—definitely not fine
6 rather large peppers, washed and seeded
3 really large onions, cut in 8 wedges (that will separate into segments as they cook)

Put the meat and all the fixin's in a machine mixing bowl with dough hook (like you use for bread making). Mix very well. Shape into 6-inch-round large balls (1 cup size) and brown on all sides, in oil and butter, turning to brown until all sides are almost (softly) crispy. You are only wanting to brown the meatballs, not cook them.

Deglaze the pan and make gravy by sprinkling a tiny bit of flour and boiling water. Add enough "leftovers" gravy that you have saved from other dishes from beef, pork and chicken to make 4 cups and pour into a large baking (glass) container, where you have placed the browned meatballs. Bake 45 minutes to 1 hour at 350 F with the sautéed peppers and onions. Cover loosely with a tinfoil tent to stop oven splatter in excess. I always place the large flat glass baking dish on a big, flat tinfoil protector that they sell at the dollar store. I place it right under the dish, not on the bottom of the oven. Particularly if you are using a gas range, do not put the tinfoil cover on the oven base. You can also bake this in a large metal roasting pan.

It's Always Turkey Time

Practice this recipe now and serve it on special holidays or as a treat for a delightful change. It's a really easy recipe. I made this for the first time nearly 40 years ago. I'm sure everyone at your house will love it.

Stuffed Breast of Turkey (Serves 4)

3 pound turkey breast
5 slices bread soaked in 1/2 cup chicken stock
1/2 pound ground veal
1 egg (beaten)
Garlic salt (or clove, if you like)
1 onion (chopped)
Fresh parsley
Salt, pepper and poultry seasoning
10 medium, large mushrooms, chopped

Sauce:

2 sticks celery (chopped)
2 cups light cream
2 eggs

Split the turkey breast, not all the way through the thickness, so it opens flat. Salt and pepper both sides. Sauté onion in clarified butter. To sautéed onion, add ground veal, salt, pepper, garlic salt and poultry seasoning. Sauté mushrooms and add to the meat mixture.

Add beaten egg to wet bread; salt and pepper. Add meat mixture and parsley to bread mixture and mix thoroughly. Spoon veal onto turkey breast, and shape veal so turkey can be rolled, so that the veal will remain more or less in a loaf-like shape in the center. Roll and tie with string (postage-package style) or truss, tucking in ends. Brush with clarified butter.

Brown in a roasting pan for 15 minutes at 425–450 F; reduce heat to 350 F and continue to cook, uncovered for 1 hour or until turkey is *just* cooked. Brush once or twice with butter while cooking.

Serve on a large platter flanked by rice steamed in chicken stock and steamed onions (quartered) and steamed carrots (quartered and cut in 2–3-inch strips), both sprinkled with sea salt. When cooked, glaze carrots with melted butter to which, 2 teaspoons of plain sugar have been added.

If you wish, you can flambé turkey before removing from the roasting pan with 2 oz. of Southern Comfort. This is not necessary but adds a delightful flavor to the sauce. Remove turkey from roaster and keep warm in the oven while making the sauce.

In the roasting pan, sauté 2 sticks of celery in a little clarified butter. Add 2 cups light cream and reduce over high heat, stirring constantly. Remove from heat and add a few spoons of hot cream to beaten eggs to adjust temperature of eggs. Add egg mixture to remaining cream and return to medium heat and *stir constantly* until mixture thickens. Be very careful or you will have scrambled eggs. Reduce heat as necessary. Enjoy!

Surprising Fruit Punch

In a large saucepan, boil 1 ½ cups of sugar and two quarts of cold water for five minutes. Cool the sugar syrup and add one cup of lemon juice, two cups of orange juice and two cups of pineapple juice. Add one 26-oz. bottle of 7UP or ginger ale. Refrigerate until ready to serve. Add vodka, gin or liquor of your choice, and float orange and lemon slices on top.

This is a great punch even as a non-alcoholic beverage. It has a combination of flavors that seems to make people think there is liquor in it even when there is not. We once made this punch to be served at a "dry" wedding. The priest kept coming back to the bowl for more, and he kept getting sillier. (He had a super personality anyway).

However, he came so often, the bride's mother saw to it that he got a large water glass to drink the punch from.

The guests still maintain the punch was "doctored." They really did enjoy themselves.

This recipe is also good for spring and summer. It's also a great poolside cooler. (Burr!)

Special Cheese Dreams

Ingredients

Italian bread
Unsalted butter
Cheddar cheese
Garlic salt
Parmesan cheese; grated
Romano cheese; grated

Slice Italian bread into slices about ½-inch thick. Allow at least two slices per person.

Butter very lightly with unsalted butter.

Cut very, very thin slices of cheddar cheese. Place these on bread slices.

Sprinkle garlic salt on ever so lightly.

Shake grated Parmesan on next, making sure to cover cheddar with a fine mist.

Top with a tiny, even shake of Romano (not very much!). The secret is to evenly distribute all the ingredients, keeping each one as light as possible.

Place on the top rack of the oven under a hot broiler for just a few minutes, until cheeses bubble and turn golden around the edges. Serve immediately. This makes a great midnight snack too.

Just Add Steak

Thinly slice sweet cooking onions until you have about a cup. Sauté in butter until the onions just start to brown. No seasoning. Place onions in a warming dish.

Increase heat (same pan) until it's very hot but not burning. Add more butter and coarsely chopped mushrooms (about a cup). Toss mushrooms quickly on high heat to sear. Do not over-cook. No seasoning. Add to the onions in the warming dish. Deglaze the pan with your favorite brandy, perhaps Asbach Uralt. Use about a quarter cup. Add liquid to mushrooms and onions dish.

While onions are cooking in a small saucepan, on medium high heat, reduce a half-cup of good, red Balsamic vinegar until it is very thick syrup. (Careful not to burn and careful because it will turn hard like sugar candy, and you don't want that to happen). Into the small saucepan, add the onion mushroom mixture and a few ounces of cold Cambozola cheese. Take away the rind first. Cover until the cheese is melted. Incorporate with a quick stir.

Serve this mixture over your favorite grilled or barbecued steak, done any way you like it, with or without garlic rub or steak spices.

If there is enough sauce for leftovers, it will keep in a covered container in the fridge for a couple of days, and will taste even better. Double or quadruple ingredients and store ahead of time for a large dinner party.

Since this recipe can be made in less than 15 minutes complete, it is a very easy recipe for entertaining with steak of any kind. Try this sauce with flank steak, thinly sliced or with strip sirloin done medium rare. It is also a great topper for any kind of rice as a side dish.

Pear Avocado Salad

This is just a salad—but what a salad!

I am debating if I have ever eaten anything as good as this in almost any food category. No kidding. It's very filling and half a large Bosc pear and a large avocado makes enough to feed four, at least.

I decided to use skinless tomatoes as a plate decoration, sliced to make "roses." But it is the dressing that is to die for. It is almost sweet in an odd way, and the combination of tastes is just wicked good. Definitely needs the lemon juice, a little extra salt (I'm not normally a big salt user) and fresh ground black pepper.

I elected to use Dijon mustard in the dressing. You can use quantities mixed however you like, including your favorite oil (must use), white Balsamic vinegar, measured in whatever suits your taste buds, the Dijon, salt, cracked black pepper, lemon juice (freshly squeezed only) to taste (check the mixture as you prepare it). I decided not to use thyme in this dressing but debated about it. But sprigs of fresh basil add to the beauty of the plate at the very end, just before serving.

Drizzle over the sliced (lengthwise) Bosc pears (peeled) and the avocado protected with lemon juice—both sliced quite thick, maybe ¼.

The roasted walnuts are not necessary but an added bonus. Spread walnut halves on a cookie sheet and place under the broiler just briefly. Watch closely. You don't want them to burn. Remove and while they are still warm, drizzle the walnuts with real maple syrup and sprinkle with salt. It's important to do that immediately. Let it rest in the open air until the salad is ready. Add it to the salad just before presenting at the table.

I used my most recent cheese-find, Raspberry cheese, but likely a really good freshly sliced Parmesan would be fine. This raspberry cheese is sort of a cross between white cheddar and Gouda. The package says it is "firm, ripened cheese; nutty and creamy, marinated in handcrafted raspberry ale." I could eat the whole block. Had a sample at the Italian pasta shop and I was completely hooked. It tastes sweet with a little salty aftertaste; crumbles a bit but can be sliced using the Dutch kaasschaaf (or a potato peeler).

This cheese is also a great late-night snack with Paris toasts (a sort of Melba toast).

If you want to make a real meal out this, add some prosciutto, sliced extremely thin, served alongside, twisted with the tomato roses, set among tufts of fresh basil. I'm thinking for summer, this would be wonderful served with freshly poached salmon (I'd douse the salmon just before serving with a little of the dressing). Perhaps even pan-seared scallops, if you like seafood. I don't think I'd do shrimps or crab with this dish, though.

Add to the eye candy by serving on beautiful black plates. Use just a tiny bit of the dressing on the plates and serve the remaining dressing on the side so people can add more if they wish. Position the pear and avocado slices in a circle around the plate.

I'm not a connoisseur of good beer, but for those who enjoy, it might go well with this salad. I think you will find that those who don't find pears among their favorite foods will fall in love with this recipe in spite of any reservations. The Bosc pears are very firm.

I can't get over how filling this food is, how absolutely simple and quick it is to prepare, and as long as you use lots of fresh-squeezed lemon on the avocado, the salad will sit covered on the counter for hours and not discolor. I also discovered a use for the leftover dressing: Marinate sole pieces just for a few minutes, then pan-fry in butter, sprinkle with fresh ground pepper and a little bit of salt, and then squeeze fresh lemon on the sole as you serve it. *Another yum!*

A Different Kind of French-Fry—Healthy Ones

Zucchini is wonderful cut like potato French fries. You'll need flour (whatever kind of flour you prefer), egg yolk wash and your favorite homemade-only breadcrumbs (not pulsed too fine). Add spices or just salt and pepper if you like, to the coarse crumbs (freeze any extra crumbs) or just use plain.

Deep fry in your favorite (fresh always) oil. Don't ever use olive oil for deep frying. The high heat breaks down the chemistry of the oil and some say it becomes a carcinogen. No sense taking chances.

Salt as soon as you remove the fries from the oil, while they are still piping hot, and place them on a paper towel to mop up any extra oil. These fries are just amazing and cook very fast.

Never walk away from a pot of hot oil on the stove. Never! It doesn't need to be a dangerous procedure. Just be careful. Do not answer the phone or the doorbell when you are deep-frying. If you turn off the heat to do so, whatever is in the pot will get soggy? But more important, if you leave the pot on the heat, you could end up with a fire.

Don't put more than necessary oil in the pot. Use a heavy pot (never a light-weight aluminum pot). Use a pot with high sides, about half full of oil. Test for the right heat by gently dropping in a cube of bread. It should immediately rise to the surface and turn golden brown if the temperature is perfect. Failing that, use an oil thermometer to test.

You often will have to adjust heat as food cooks, because the food is redistributing the heat. That's how it is supposed to be, so if you are not familiar with deep-frying, it's okay. Don't add too much food. Fry in small quantities. Keep food warm with a tinfoil tent, but be careful, because the food will continue to cook it its own heat and you don't want to create steam. The food needs to breathe.

When the breadcrumbs are a nice golden color, the zucchini is done. Sometimes I put a sprinkle of Parmesan and Romano mixed grated cheese in the breadcrumbs and add some favorite spices, like a pinch of dried thyme and garlic salt. Enjoy!

If you enjoy spicy things, sprinkle cooked fries with cayenne pepper while the fries are still hot. Good, and good for you, but beware…the cayenne is hot, so if you have never used it, be very careful…use just a bit. Cayenne pepper is great, by the way, on egg salad. Actually, it's fabulous!

Butter Is Better

You will find all sorts of uses for these delicious butters. Roll them in wax paper to make a shape like a sausage. Tuck in the ends of the wax paper and store in the coldest part of the refrigerator. You can easily slice them in chunks once the butter is really firm. Then you are ready to serve to surprise last-minute guests.

They are super nice in a freshly made crepe, topped with dollops of stiffly beaten sweetened whipped cream. You can add powdered dark cocoa to the whipped cream for a change of taste. You can also make chocolate crepes by adding powered dark chocolate to your favorite crepe recipe.

Economy Butter Cream

1 cup soft unsalted butter

1 cup icing sugar

1 egg yolk

Flavoring (vanilla, coffee, strawberry)

Beat all ingredients together until fluffy, about 4-5 min.

For the whipped cream, add ¼ cup icing sugar instead of sugar. The vanilla is necessary; use real vanilla always, not the artificial one.

Add ¼ cup icing sugar instead of sugar and vanilla

Strawberry Butter

1 cup butter (soft but still firm)

2 cup powdered sugar

1 egg yolk

1 cup sliced fresh firm strawberries

Beat butter with powdered sugar and egg yolk on high until fluffy.

Purée berries—just pulse a couple of times (you don't want soup consistency). Fold slowly to butter mixture.

Makes 2½ cup fruit butter. Add your favorite nuts if desired.

Serve either of these butters on slices of your favorite pound cake, or between layers of a homemade torte.

My Special Bell Pepper Marinade

Core and seed mixed colored, quartered, medium-large peppers. Use the tops—just pop out the "handle," and toss it in the trash. Always cut a pepper from the outside (skin side) inward; never start to cut on the inner flesh side because that can easily bruise the skins, sometimes making them bitter. Split a medium small white onion into quarters. Save three quarters for another use, and open one quarter into pieces.

Soak the pepper pieces and onion in a half-cup of corn oil and a generous splash of white balsamic vinegar. Add a couple of turns of course ground black pepper (no salt yet), a couple of small pieces of garlic split in half and a half lemon, cut into four pieces to expose the membrane juices. Sprinkle on a tiny bit (Careful!) of dried thyme.

Cover the container with plastic wrap and let it marinate on the counter for a few hours, tossing it every now and then.

Remove the peppers and onion and save them in a separate dish. Toss away the lemon pieces. In the next day or two, when you barbecue, place the peppers and onion on a barbecue cooking container that is punched full of holes and barbecue the veggies to serve with your meat or chicken course.

Pour the marinade into a jar and shake vigorously. Make sure the lid is on tight.

This sauce can be used as an absolutely amazing salad dressing over any kind of lettuce or lettuce mixture. You can drizzle it over barbecue chicken slices that are arranged on lettuce leaves just at serving time.

You can use it to marinade raw chicken or steak before barbecuing, but then you cannot use the remainder due to the meat juices joining the sauce. But, fresh from the jar, you can brush it on meat or chicken while cooking. If you are using as a marinade, just spoon enough into the holding dish to do the job so you can save the rest in the jar for another use. The taste is beyond description.

The jar will keep in the fridge for several days, covered. Shake well before each use.

Try something a little different: Sprinkle (just a bit) of the sauce over a bowl of split strawberries and peaches together and serve as a main course side dish, on a large lettuce leaf or spinach leaves. Or, add a little to chopped fresh juicy tomatoes (salt and peppered) mixed with home-made crispy bacon pieces and a tiny bit of chopped onion.

Try marinating whole sea scallops in this sauce, just for a minute, turning them once and then barbecue as usual. You will find lots of uses for this charmer.

Strawberries: A Special Super Easy Dessert

Try this: sprinkle sugar to taste over quite-ripe chopped fresh berries, then cover with ordinary two-per-cent milk. Let stand a few minutes, then mash and stir. Refrigerate. A chemical reaction takes place and the mixture begins to thicken. It tastes even better the next day.

Serve it in stem glasses or in a shrimp cocktail glass with a bit of crushed ice in the base of the container part. Decorate with a sprig of mint and any kind of berries.

More Strawberries—Leftovers

Here's another great use for strawberries: Make the strawberries and milk mixture as noted. Make extra. Leave it in the fridge for a couple days. Then, put the berry mix in a metal dish or one that is freezer safe. Freeze until solid.

Place the container on the counter for about 20 minutes. You don't want it to thaw, but it will get hard as a brick and you will think you can do nothing with it. When you are able to remove the frozen mixture from the container, break or chop the frozen berry mix into a few large chunks. Place it in a food processor and whirr—pulse until a solid mush forms, sort of like ice cream thickness, scraping down the sides of the machine dish.

Place it in, ideally, a metal container with a cover. I use a plum pudding container that has a cover. Re-freeze. Now you have a semi freddo. You can use this dessert like an ice cream dish. Call it a sherbet or a sorbet, or you can use it as a palette cleanser between courses.

Try placing the mold upside-down on a large cake plate. Release the frozen mold. Cover it with whipped cream and decorate with fresh berries (any kind), or try covering the mold with stiffly beaten egg white. Then flambé it with a portable gas flash torch at the table.

You can make the semi freddo in individual muffin tin trays and decorate each one individually. First freeze the mixture in the muffin trays, whir each one individually in a food processor and repack into the muffin trays. These keep (covered) in the freezer for a long, long time just like ice cream. Now you have an instant gourmet treat when company comes.

Save That Pumpkin

Traditionally, after Halloween millions of pumpkins find their new homes: in garbage bins. Jack-o-lanterns are the symbol of All hallows' Eve, or All Saints' Day, across our nation.

The celebration of Halloween is credited to the rites of the druids' celebration of the day of Saman when, traditionally, the Lord of Death called together the souls of the wicked who had died during the year. Thankfully, the modern celebrations lean toward the old Roman festivals, held in honor of Pomona, the goddess of fruit.

Try adding pumpkin pie filling to your favorite tomato soup cake recipe or to your favorite spice cake recipe. Pumpkin can also be done up in chutneys and or preserves, for a really special mid-winter treat.

Halloween is not celebrated in England or Continental Europe, so children of families who recently moved here from overseas will be in for great fun and excitement every year always on the same date, on the night of October 31.

Surprise a new neighbor from another culture with a freshly baked pumpkin pie, to honor the post-Halloween celebrations.

The recipe that follows is from a mid-1970s column, but it's a favorite around our house and I feel confident you will make it an annual favorite too—serving it not just on Halloween, but on many other festive occasions. By the way, don't let the candle char the inside of the pumpkin too much.

The pumpkin is a relative of the squash and it too grows on a vine. It is a fruit, as is the tomato, as well as the avocado; not a vegetable. One cup of canned pumpkin contains 7.750 international units of Vitamin A, which although only half as much as in a cup of raw carrots, is high compared to other fruits. There are only 75 calories per cup of canned pumpkin, so if you are dieting, leave the pastry and just eat the filing.

This recipe calls for fresh, baked pumpkin; therefore, allow plenty of time for preparation. It is not difficult to make. Even if you have never made a pumpkin pie before, there's no time like right now to turn on your oven and add this to your recipe box.

Pastry

2 cup flour
1 cup unsalted butter
½ cup sugar
½ teaspoon vanilla
2 egg yolks

Mix all ingredients together and spread on to the bottom and sides of Pyrex pie plates. Prick the pastry with a fork. Bake for 8–10 minutes at 400 degrees. Cool.

This recipe will cover one 9-inch and one 11-inch pie plate.

Filling

5 cups "baked" pumpkin
1–3/4 cup packed brown sugar
1–1/2 teaspoon salt
2 teaspoon cinnamon
1 teaspoon ginger
1 teaspoon nutmeg
Sprinkle each of mace (which is the flower of the nutmeg, having a sweeter taste), cardamom and ground cloves
3 whole eggs; beaten
1–3/4 cup milk and 1 cup water

Bake one medium-size pumpkin on a cookie sheet, in a 325-degree oven for about 1–1/4 hours, or until it has the consistency of a baked potato when you prick the skin with a fork. Prick the pumpkin in several spots near top before baking to prevent it from rupturing.

After the pumpkin is baked, slice off its top. If you can get the seeds out without too much trouble with a slotted spoon, do so. Otherwise slice the pumpkin vertically into large pieces and pare away the skin and scrape off the seeds. Mash the flesh of the pumpkin with a potato masher or break it down in a Cuisinart. It is too coarse at this stage for a regular blender.

Heat the pumpkin flesh in a stainless steel or coated cast iron pot, on medium heat for about 10 minutes. Preheat the oven to 400 F degrees.

Mix sugar and spices together and stir into the hot pumpkin. Add beaten eggs to water and milk. Add this mixture to the pumpkin. Purée in the blender. Fill the prepared pastry shells (quite full) and bake at 400 degrees for 15 minutes. Turn down the heat to 300 F degrees and continue baking for 45 minutes. Cool. Serve at room temperature with whipped cream.

This filling freezes well, if you have time to double up on the recipe for later use.

Prepare the pastry shells several hours ahead, even the day before, so that the pastry is completely cool. Paint the pastry with egg white wash before filling to help the pastry stay dry. You might want to drizzle the whipped cream dollop at serving time, with a little maple syrup. A sprig of mint leaves on the side of the serving plate adds a nice touch.

My Incredible Marsala Chicken (Gets Magnificent Reviews)

3–4 pounds cut-up chicken
½—¾ cup Marsala dessert wine
1 cup boiling water
1 tablespoon salt
1 teaspoon thyme; crushed, not ground
½ teaspoon sweet basil and a sprinkle of Italian seasoning
1 teaspoon garlic salt
1 tablespoon unsalted butter
¼ cup corn oil
Preheat oven to 400 F

Wash the chicken pieces thoroughly under cold running water. Dry on a paper towel.

Melt the butter with oil in a skillet and allow it to turn golden in color. Turn down the heat slightly, but keep the skillet very hot. Place the chicken pieces skin side down in the skillet and do not move them around. Put in only as many pieces as the skillet will comfortably hold.

When the chicken pieces are quite brown, turn them with a pair of tongs. Allow the bone side of the chicken only about half the length of time to brown as you did for the skinned side.

Remove the chicken pieces from the skillet with tongs and place them in a roasting pan that has a cover, placing pieces one on top of another if necessary. When all the chicken pieces are browned on both sides, deglaze the skillet with the Marsala wine, scraping the bottom free of bits of stuck-on skin. Add boiling water and allow it to decrease in volume by about one-third.

Sprinkle herbs and salts over the chicken pieces and then pour liquid from the skillet over top. Cover and place in the oven. Turn the temperature down to 325 F and allow the chicken to cook for about 1–1/2 hours.

Remove the chicken pieces from the hot roasting pan and place on a platter. Keep them warm while you make gravy.

If there is excess fat floating on top of drippings in the roasting pan, pour it off or spoon it off. Make a paste from 3 tablespoon of flour and some of the drippings, in a small dish. Gradually add the remaining liquid from the roasting pan. Stir until married. Return the gravy to the roasting pan or a small pot and cook, stirring constantly, on top of the stove until thickened. This mixture must be completely cooked in order to break down the flour and make it digestible.

This for people who like old-fashioned flour gravy. I prefer to scald cream until it thickens and stir it into the drippings, folding gently. But careful about re-heating so it doesn't curdle.

Serve the gravy in a separate container.

Serve this fabulous chicken with fluffy white Basmati rice or mashed, whipped potatoes.

Garnish the serving platter with large sprigs of parsley and lemon wedges.

Bonus: The bouquet that fills the house for about 48 hours is as delicious as the meal.

Finish up the meal with a complementary **Marsala dessert**.

Try making the so-simple sabayon or zabaglione. Make it the regular way with your favorite white wine, but just before serving, spritz it with Marsala and fold.

Serve in stemmed shot glasses, sitting on odd leftover saucers that don't necessarily match (you saved them and you didn't know why), with a sprig of fresh basil and topped with brandy-soaked fresh half-strawberries. This dessert is best served at room temperature. If you have tiny little coffee-spoons, this is a great opportunity to use them, placed delicately on the side of the saucer. You can place a lace doily on the saucer for special occasions to add a little glam.

Multi-Fruit Dessert

Here's a multi-fruit dessert to keep on hand all year round:

2 medium large Bosc pears; cored and peeled

1/2 medium large red delicious apple, cored and peeled

1 medium large peach, peeled, pit removed

1/2 medium, medium ripe banana

Chop the fruit in large pieces. Chop in the blender. With the blender running, add 1/2 cup of white sugar and 1 cup of half-and-half cream.

Keep the blender running for about a minute. The mixture will thicken. Stir in a teaspoon of peach or pear brandy or your favorite brandy.

Pour it into a bowl that can go in the freezer. I use a metal plum pudding container that has a cover.

There are a couple of different ways to serve. When frozen solid, remove from the container bowl and position it upside down on a cake server plate that you have made cold in the fridge. Use whipped egg whites for meringue. With a spatula, cover the frozen fruit mixture.

With a handheld decorating torch, singe the meringue till just lightly brown. Work quickly.

Position mandarin orange segments around the plate edge, just as you are ready to serve. Keep it in the coldest part of the fridge briefly until ready to serve.

Using a sharp serrated knife, cut in wedges. Lay the wedges on their sides and drizzle just a few drops fresh really good maple syrup.

Serve as salad: Split a quite ripe avocado in half and remove the pit. Spritz with white balsamic vinegar and olive oil and fresh ground black cracked peppercorns.

Using an ice cream scoop, position a round of the frozen fruit mix in the hole where the pit was.

Serve on a plate of a mix of shredded romaine and iceberg lettuce with a few large cold shrimp strategically positioned around the avocado half.

Sprinkle with fresh roasted walnut halves that, while still hot, you have drizzled with real maple syrup and sprinkled with coarse salt. If you fancy a little heat, dust the sugared walnuts with a little finely ground cayenne pepper.

This is a mock semi-fredo, or sorbet-like dessert. There are no eggs in it. Sort of a cross between sorbet and semi-fredo. I'm thinking you could easily make this in individual bite sizes to pop in your mouth, in either tiny paper cups that you peel off, or in mini metal muffin tins.

Tap to release. Serve in a puddle of zabaglione perhaps, surrounded by fresh raspberries and or blueberries or even sweet, seedless white grapes. A tiny dollop of whipped cream on top, and again drizzle with really good quality maple syrup.

Note: Here's an easy peel for peaches: cut an X on the bottom of the peach and cover for a couple of minutes with boiling water. Let stand, then dip in ice water or just really cold water briefly. The skin will slip right off.

This is a quick and easy way to remove tomato skins too.

This dessert takes less than 10 minutes to prepare and it's terrific to keep on hand to serve to unexpected guests. Instant gourmet.

It "travels" as a take-along in a freezer carry pocket like a frozen bag used for wine. This dish is beyond simple to make and tastes incredible. It keeps, covered, in the freezer for a long time.

Use Cream to Thicken Soup

Behold the cow! Not only does this lowly animal provide us with beef for our tables, a most valuable source of protein, but dairy cattle the world over are the suppliers of perhaps one of the only products that, alone, can sustain life for long periods of time—milk, in its various forms, and cream.

Whenever I make cream soups, I never thicken them with flour, always with cream. If you are counting calories, use cereal cream instead of heavy cream. But if you figure 800 to 1,000 calories per cup of heavy cream and divide this by six servings, the calories intake is not so great.

For those of you who are calorie counting, use my recipes for those special occasions when you prepare a treat for yourself, or for when you are entertaining.

I always bake and cook, with unsalted butter, rarely lard (only for certain requirements), and never with margarine, although for certain recipes I do use corn oil.

Contrary to all the hype about corn and its mismanagement, Mazola Corn Oil is cholesterol free and due to its high heat capacity, is still an excellent oil to use for deep frying. I use it exclusively when deep frying. There are plenty of negative discussions about Canola Oil and personally, I have never used it. I just didn't have a good feeling about it, right from the beginning.

There are times when margarine will substitute for butter in some folks' kitchens, but I was so turned off by the initial wartime version of the margarine, when orange food-coloring was added to make it look like butter, that I never got past that. It was never used in my home growing up. I was a war baby and recall my mother trading her butter ration coupons with friends and neighbors to be able to bake and cook with real butter. We even had butter on baked potatoes.

She gave up other ration coupons—things she didn't use because butter was so important. If you prefer to use an alternative, or if you are calorie counting or budget watching, alternatives are applicable to nearly every general recipe, but do bear in mind that substitutes are substitutes, and a recipe that you enjoyed at a friend's house will not taste the same when you make it if you use substitutes in the recipe.

I recently read an article where an economist advocated replacing cream in soup with milk and then proceeded to say if the soup was not creamy enough, to add butter. False economy both dollar-wise and calorie-wise.

Just use the cream. The soup will go just as far and taste so much better. The money some people enjoy spending eating out regularly, I would rather spend in my own kitchen and I feel we eat better for less this way. And more importantly, I know what is in the food, to a greater degree.

Yes, it takes time, but time spent preparing meals is the ultimate multi-tasking opportunity. You can watch television, read your favorite magazine, clean the fridge, knit or crochet—all while you are in the kitchen. This time each day or even a couple of times a week is an ideal family time, teaching children how the kitchen works. Meal prep time is also an opportunity for bonding between mates, even if the mate doesn't cook. Help with clean up counts big time.

These recipes are my own concoctions and are so simple and so delightful that you'll enjoy making (and eating) them regularly. If you enjoy cream soups in the upcoming cold, wet weather days ahead, yes, you can freeze them. But freeze the base, prior to adding the cream. Take it out of the freezer the day before you plan to eat it and let it thaw in the fridge, ideally.

Scald the cream, and let it rise and fall three times. Never take your eyes off it. Never leave the stove. And certainly, never leave the room. Scalding overflow makes a terrible stinky mess.

Let the cream settle and gently fold in your soup base, using a wooden spoon. If the base is lumpy, gently whisk away the lumps. Do not beat the mixture. Return to soft heat and stir until ready to serve. It shouldn't separate if done properly. Reheating is possible once the cream is enveloped with the base, but only very carefully because it will burn. Perhaps use a double boiler if necessary, to reheat, or holding temperature to serve if required.

Tomato Mushroom Bisque

Sauté six large red tomatoes from your garden. Mash with a potato masher. Or, sauté one large tin of whole tomatoes in hot butter until liquid is reduced by a third. Add a generous pinch of thyme and parsley along with a sprinkle of ground oregano. Salt and pepper. Turn it into a heavy soup pot.

In same skillet, sauté in plenty of bubbly hot butter and one pound of button mushrooms, quartered. Only sauté the mushrooms for a couple of minutes, on very high heat. Do not salt. Sprinkle a little pepper and dried thyme. Add to the tomatoes.

Stir three cups of homemade chicken stock into the soup pot and bring it to a boil. Reduce by one third. Deglaze the skillet with a few tablespoons of any kind of wine or brandy and add to the soup.

Cover and let it stand until ready to serve. Reheat but do not boil.

Add two cups of hot, light, scalded (cereal) cream and stir. Makes six generous servings.

As an alternative, pulse this soup with a handheld blender, leaving it lumpy in texture. Serve in a rustic bowl, with really crunchy croutons on top, when bringing to the table and add a dollop of sour cream as a special treat. Drizzle the sour cream with real maple syrup. Do not stir.

Note: Now for a really different soup, use fresh green tomatoes from your garden. Sprinkle with crunchy, fresh, homemade bacon bits. Just before serving grate some real Parmesan cheese over the green tomato mushroom bisque. Genuine yum!

I thought some of you might find this

https://www.youtube.com/watch?v=6EeIQcWex5w&sns=em interesting—I'm old enough to remember much of this—yes, there was rationing here in Canada, too, although not as restricted, but still "the law."

Spectacular Barbecue Serving Sauce

(A reader who made this recipe said: "This is so wonderful; I'll never buy ketchup again.")

Don't throw away that leftover red half-tomato. **(You could substitute white tomato, yellow or orange tomato.)**

Nothing much ever goes to waste in my kitchen. I had a large red tomato and I used half of it for a plain old-fashioned tomato sandwich.

I don't like tomato skins so I had scorched it with boiling water, making the X on the bottom so as to let the skin just slip off. A couple of nice thick slices made a great sandwich.

So, I made barbecue sauce with the leftovers. You can easily double or even quadruple this recipe.

2 tablespoons finely chopped white onion

Pinch of dried thyme

1/2 medium red tomato; chopped

1 teaspoon chopped fresh parsley

1 teaspoon finely chopped fresh basil

2 tablespoon white Balsamic vinegar

Minced crushed garlic clove

I tablespoon best maple syrup

Salt, fresh cracked pepper

1 tablespoon plum jam (my special German confit made with Italian blue plums)

1 tablespoon orange marmalade

1 fig (chopped or mashed), marinated in brandy

1/2 teaspoon mustard

Grated orange and lemon rind

Sauté the onion—careful not to burn it; just translucent. Add pinch of dried thyme. Then add tomato, herbs, vinegar and garlic. Stir and then add the syrup. Adjust seasonings. Mash using fork tines.

When the mixture has cooked down and thickened, add 1 tablespoon homemade plum jam, (or favorite store bought), 1 tablespoon orange marmalade and one marinated-in-brandy black mission fig. Stir in the mustard.

Mash and stir the finished mixture. Stir in the rind.

Cover the container with plastic wrap as well as its cover, in a storage jar in the coldest area of the fridge, for up to several weeks. Keep it airtight.

The flavor of the good brandied fig will enhance the overall wonderful taste. And the fragrance permeates the kitchen.

Use on barbecued butterfly center-cut pork chops, barbecued lamb chops or barbecued fish. Top meat or fish with this sauce just minutes before serving, while still on the barbecue. Be careful not to burn it. Serve immediately.

This sauce is also suitable for barbecued large portobello mushrooms. They taste like steak.

Remove the stem. Paint the mushrooms with just a little olive oil on both sides. Sprinkle with pepper on the inside side only. Salt after cooking is finished.

Barbecue for three to four minutes on each side on medium high heat. Spoon a little sauce on the stem side. Serve it whole or sliced in thick slices. Truly wonderful!

This sauce even enhances sautéed liver. As with other uses, paint on a little sauce only during last few minutes. Since the sauce is sweet, it will become sticky and easily burn.

Try this sauce on Rock Cornish hens, too.

Cherry Tomatoes Exposé

Here's a great way to prepare cherry tomatoes—yellow and red in balsamic and soya sauce.

First split the bigger ones in half. Use dark good balsamic vinegar (1:3) and your favorite oil cooked on top of the stove with a little brown sugar and a little soya sauce.

Add a pinch of good mustard, stirred in. When it thickens just slightly and coats a spoon, it is ready to use.

Fabulous on cherry tomatoes with baby spinach leaves. Enjoy! So yum…

Grilled Shrimp Kabobs and Tapas

Make plenty; you can never make too much of this treat.

Rinse and clean some medium-large shrimp. Leave the shells on.

Split the back shell with a sharp serrated knife or kitchen shears, and using the long tines of a kitchen fork, gently scrape out any black vein. Leave the shells on, otherwise fully intact, tail on.

Skewer each shrimp using flat, pointed, wooden skewers, first pushing the skewer through the flat thick end of each shrimp and continuing through the less thick part.

Allow six to eight shrimp per skewer, pushing the shrimp so they barely touch one another, lining them up flat.

Mount the skewers on a clean, hot oiled grill, positioning the handle portion of each skewer on a roll of tinfoil along the edge of the barbecue grate. This portion of each skewer acts as a handle.

Using a spray bottle for each, spray the shrimp with your favorite white wine or white balsamic vinegar. Then spray with high quality "Spanish" olive oil. Sprinkle the shrimp with plenty of coarse salt and grains of pepper. (Spanish olive oil is quite different than Italian olive oil.)

Be very careful not to overcook the shelled shrimp. As soon as shrimp turns opaque it is cooked. Ideally about two minutes each side.

Turn the shrimp kabobs and repeat the sprays, salt and pepper. The shells will char and give off a wonderful aroma that might call in your neighbors unexpectedly.

Don't forget that food continues to cook when removed from the cooking source heat.

Absolutely don't overcook seafood of any type; it will get rubbery. Awful. Nearly not edible. But if you do happen to overcook, don't waste the seafood. Freeze it and save it for another recipe. Never waste food.

Start your cooking process again; refrigerate the overcooked portions and put them through your kitchen machine another day.

Remove the shrimp kabobs from the grill and rest, shells still intact, on a heavy stone or glazed plate.

Spray large thick pieces of black olive bread that you have rubbed with garlic clove with Spanish olive oil, and grill both sides. The bread will be the basis of your tapas.

Before cooking your shrimp, prepare your roasted vegetable paste spread by grilling your favorite vegetables, skins on, until just barely fork tender.

When the skins turn black, remove the vegetables from the grill, remove seeds, chop into medium-size pieces and place the vegetable pieces in a kitchen machine, using a sharp blade.

Whir until just coarse. Add a little dried Parmesan cheese, a tiny bit of sour cream, salt, pepper, a smashed garlic clove or a bit of oven roasted garlic, a little Spanish olive oil and a squirt of white balsamic vinegar. Add a tiny bit of smoked paprika and or cayenne pepper powder, to taste.

I prefer to leave the charred skins on the vegetable mix, but you might prefer to scrape off the roasted skins.

I use bell peppers, mixed colors, firm eggplant, sliced Spanish onion and zucchini, along with whole large grilled firm red tomato.

The coarse spread can be kept for a couple of days, covered, in a glass container, refrigerated.

Spread a heaping tablespoon of the vegetable mix on each piece of grilled black olive bread. Top with a round or two of black peppercorns, and add fresh grated parmesan cheese.

The tapas are a wonderful accompaniment to the grilled shrimp kabobs. Serve with a robust Spanish wine.

It's an ideal Sunday brunch or a late-night celebration of any kind, all year round.

If you have an indoor grill such as a Jenn Air type stovetop grill, this process even works indoors in cold weather seasons. Keep your overhead fan running.

Invite your guests to join you on the patio, or in your kitchen in off seasons.

Make plenty; you can never make too much of this treat.

To plate, serve with frozen grapes. The grapes will pop in your mouth. If serving on a side table, decorate a large serving plate displaying the grilled shrimp kabobs surrounded by candied green seedless grapes and large black olives. And my all-time favorite: Brandy marinated figs. Provide lots of party stick-picks.

OR: Dip grapes in egg whites and plunge in a bowl of plain white sugar. Shake off excess. Refrigerate until serving. Serve alongside dark chocolate dipped whole strawberries, all mounted on a bed of fresh basil leaves. It's a feast for the eyes too.

Special Egg Salad Holiday Treat

At some point in our discussions a while ago, we got onto the topic of eggs. If you know you should eat fish a couple of times each week (and some nutritionists recommend eating salmon or tuna, even from a tin, twice each week) but you just can't bring yourself to eat fresh fish, try this for a little something different.

Make egg salad with nothing in it other than a little salt, pepper and mayo. Personally, I prefer finely mashed egg salad, rather than the course chunky variety.

Mash drained tinned tuna or red salmon and add a quarter cup to your egg salad. You can use fresh cooked or tinned fish. Smoked salmon works well, too.

This mix makes a great appetizer treat, served on your favorite crackers (maybe sprinkle a little paprika on top), or on a slice of cucumber as the base (sprinkle a little, fresh only, dill on top). It works in cucumber "boats" too.

If you want to get creative, serve the fishy egg salad on a washed, crispy endive leaf. The mixture is even good as everyday lunchbox sandwiches (wrapped in plastic wrap or tightly covered travel box).

You will come back to this easy-fix time and time again. It makes another of those quick and easy, grab and run, real food items you can pack for a lunch or a picnic also. As a real estate professional on the run, keep this handy, good-for-you food at the ready. You will find many uses for this yummy treat, even in the holiday season or as an after the game treat.

The egg-fish mixture will keep, covered, in the fridge for a couple of days. Teens will actually eat it and the little people will ask for more. Slice regular white bread sandwiches for little ones in strips for a treat; maybe even remove the crusts. Introduce an olive or a chunk of pineapple, maybe even a piece of avocado spritzed with lemon, strategically positioned with a fancy color toothpick.

If you recall the days of high tea, this is a perfect opportunity to use open-face sandwiches or tiered ones, cut in small, crustless strips. If you feel really creative, use a star or serrated edge cookie cutter to make fancy sandwiches.

Decorate the serving plate with sprigs of fresh watercress. The English even make wonderful watercress sandwiches. Add thinly sliced cucumber to your sandwich list. Everything old is new again, all year 'round.

A Perfect Picnic: Chicken Legs and Coleslaw

Marinate chicken legs for a few hours in your favorite oil and white balsamic vinegar 3:1 and a little Dijon mustard. No salt or pepper.

Dredge lightly in flour, dip in beaten egg, and then roll in freshly made loose (not fine) breadcrumbs. Use your preferred seasoning. I like a generous pinch of dried thyme and a little salt and pepper in the crumbs, but just plain is fine, too. (Panko flakes work if you prefer.)

Brown in hot oil on the stovetop in a deep skillet, turning to seal all sides, for a few minutes.

Remove from the skillet and place upright in a baking pan, sized to accommodate all the pieces.

Cover tightly with heavy tinfoil (shiny side in); poke a couple of steam release small holes in the tinfoil and bake at medium high heat (350–375 F) for about a half hour.

Remove the tinfoil and use it to make an open tent to cover while the chicken rests.

These fabulous chicken legs can be served immediately or counter cooled and refrigerated to serve at room temperature or cool the next day. Amazing finger food.

Serve with your favorite salad.

These chicken legs are super picnic fare or great to take along to a potluck meal. You likely will never want to eat chicken legs prepared any other way again.

A variation: Try making a large turkey leg using this recipe. Gauge your cooking time according to the size, as you normally would.

Always test poultry to make sure it is completely cooked—but *absolutely* not overdone, as poultry will get chewy and tough.

Coleslaw Extraordinaire

Cabbage is touted as a natural healer food, often recommended to keep a liver healthy. It's often said to heal a stomach disorder. A bowl of this dish can make a whole meal in all seasons. Served with a buttered roll, it makes a delightful lunch. It's also an ideal picnic food.

As a side dish, accompanying any meal, it's wonderful, but fish and chips are just not complete without coleslaw.

It's best to always make your own coleslaw and it can be done in no time. Keep some on hand for a go-to favorite. For those who grow their own vegetables, this will be a fabulous standby to have on hand.

Shred cabbage and very fresh, sweet, raw carrots, very fine; almost minced. A mandolin works well, set to fine, but be extra careful. The blades are very sharp.

Marinate shredded cabbage and just a little bit of carrot for a few hours in white balsamic vinegar and white sugar mix, 3:1. Keep the marinade on hand in fridge, but let it come to room temperature prior to using. Shake to emulsify. Use enough to completely cover the cabbage and carrots. Cover the bowl while the vegetables marinate with a fresh tea towel and let rest. Keep the air out.

Drain completely, wrapped, and squeezed in cheesecloth. Add your favorite mayonnaise, the real thing, ideally homemade, that you keep on hand in the fridge. Some people like less sauce, others more.

Sprinkle with a little salt and just a tiny bit of fresh cracked pepper. Keep refrigerated until ready to serve once the mayo is added.

Never let anything containing mayonnaise sit on the counter indefinitely—and certainly never let it sit in the sun, if serving outside in hot weather.

Keep food that is to be served outside in a travel cooler until ready to serve. Keep covered, preferably in a glass container. You don't want a chemical reaction between plastic and vinegar.

Likewise, never store any food that has vinegar in it in plastic containers.

Eggs can go bad in hot or humid air. And mayo typically has eggs or egg yolks.

Homemade mayo will keep, covered airtight in a glass bottle, in the fridge, for at least six months.

For a little change up for your friends or family expecting a little gourmet extra, at the last minute, stir in a smidgen of freshly grated horseradish. Or a minuscule bit of Dijon mustard. Not much of either, because you don't want to overpower the already wonderful taste.

Make lots because someone will want a take-home serving, no doubt.

Another keeper recipe—even for those who say they don't cook.

Caramelized Onions on Long Baguette

Good all year round, I also serve this treat for Christmas Day family brunch. It doesn't need any accompaniment.

Slice several large Spanish onions into thin rounds, about six to eight cups. For purposes of elegant presentation, cross-cut works best, as rings.

In a high-quality, heavy-bottom, large, low, stainless-steel skillet, using Mazola Corn Oil (it's cholesterol free— and I'm aware of the corn modification situation), and unsalted butter, a generous sprinkle of crushed dry thyme, a tiny bit of salt and two or three whole garlic cloves (mash them when soft; they become so very mild)—over medium heat, sweat the onions stirring gently so the mixture glazes, carefully scraping the bottom of the skillet.

Be patient, this takes a while. Stay with the stove; adjust the heat as necessary until caramelization is complete. You don't want brown or burnt onions.

When the onions are translucent and the white onion has caramelized in color, stir in a tablespoon of brown sugar and a tablespoon of good real maple syrup.

If you have stored fresh figs in brandy or cognac, as I have noted in other columns, mash one into the skillet mixture for a divine addition for the palette of your gourmet friends.

When onions are perfectly "just" cooked (not mushy), and the pan is still very hot, add a half cup of your favorite brandy or cognac.

Carefully flambé and burn off the alcohol. Stir gently. Add freshly grated cracked black peppercorns. Sprinkle with grated Parmesan cheese. Don't continue to stir.

Under the broiler, brown four long, split fresh baguettes, sprinkled with your best olive oil on the cut side. Don't let them dry out. Remove when the tops turn brown.

Using a long-handled fork with long tines, or using tongs, lift out the onion rings, and mound the split baguettes generously high with the caramelized onions and serve hot; split each long baguette in half lengths, cut wide angle on the diagonal.

Each half of half will be a serving. Serve on oval plates if you have them. Looks great on a dark chocolate or black plate. Decorate with a handful of fresh parsley and a lemon wedge. It is a large bread serving, covered mounded high with the sautéed onions.

As an alternative, making this delight even richer, sprinkle grated Mozzarella cheese on top and broil to bubble, for just a few seconds, only when ready to serve.

A tankard of your favorite beer will be well received with this delicious brunch. Good all year round, I also serve this treat for Christmas Day family brunch. It doesn't need any accompaniment.

If you want to serve this amazing treat as a main dish meal, just serve a great salad on the side. The onion presentation is very filling.

Remember, first we eat with our eyes.

Note: For a summertime treat, go back to my barbecue sauce recipe where you will find the barbecue potatoes and onions done in tinfoil papillote. Use onions cooked this way, on barbecued baguettes, served in this manner alongside your barbecue steak.

http://www.remonline.com/recipes-busy-sales-reps-spectacular-barbecue-serving-sauce/

Meat Sauce Gravy

Of the thousands of recipes out there that use ground beef as a base staple, it's safe to say that this will likely be your favorite from now on. This mix is a great budget conscientious dollar extender. It feeds many at no great expense.

Seriously brown a half pound of ground beef (fresh, not frozen, preferably), in a bit of butter in a heavy pot, on medium high heat.

Constantly stir the beef but let it stick to the pot a little so it really browns well, scraping the bottom of the pot, as the ground beef cooks. You don't want to overcook the beef. When it's not pink, it's done.

Remember that browned butter takes on a really nutty flavor.

Add a pinch of salt and a little pepper and just a sprinkle of grated nutmeg.

Add a tablespoon of beurre manié that you have prepared mashing equal parts of butter and flour. This is a rare occasion when I use flour.

Gently work the manié into the well-browned beef. I stress well-browned, because it so affects the flavor. Less than well-browned lacks the outstanding taste, so be sure it's nearly toasted, because you are using medium high heat, but you don't want crispy beef. Again, that produces a less desirable end product.

This process will completely thicken with no lumps. Gradually stir in three cups of well-seasoned homemade chicken stock. Turn the heat down to low.

Add a cup of scalded cream and gently stir, scraping any stuck-on bits from the bottom of the pot. You want thick yummy sauce but not gooey. It must be able to pour. Adjust the seasoning if necessary. The sauce will continue to thicken in its own heat until served.

This fabulous meat sauce gravy will become an instant favorite at your house.

Ladled over mashed, whipped potatoes, you will have to control your senses not to overindulge. Be sure to make more than enough potatoes. There won't be leftovers.

This mix is also a great base for baked pot pies.

You simply can't believe how simple this is to prepare. Everyone from big baby to old grandpa will ask for this meal many times, again.

Here are some additional gourmet edits for this basic recipe:

You can wilt (sweat) a little finely minced onion and stir it into nearly finished sauce, but be careful because the onion can overtake the gentle beef flavor. Use only a teaspoon, perhaps.

For a spectacular gourmet different touch, stir in a little Dijon mustard, or a little fresh grated horseradish.

Try a little oven-roasted mashed garlic added while the sauce is still hot, if your family enjoys a little extended creativity.

This recipe keeps well if anyone is late arriving to the table. But the best way to reheat is using a bain-marie, to keep the consistency.

Spoon the sauce over the mashed potatoes just prior to serving. Any of your favorite vegetables as an accompaniment will work well.

When my children were growing up, this was a family favorite and one that I ate in basic form regularly.

I grew up not being allowed in the kitchen. It was my mother's domain.

The works in progress, although simple and certainly not creative gourmet by any definition, always smelled wonderful and everything tasted great, but beneath the surface I wanted so much to be there.

Occasionally, I was permitted to "stand back" and watch. She seemed to find it curious that a child might be interested. And then there was the possibility that a hair might arrive uninvited into the kitchen. Never.

I replicate her style of never leaving a mess in the kitchen. I don't recall ever seeing a messy kitchen. It's so much easier to clean up as you go and it adds no extra time at all to the experience; it is multi-tasking at its finest.

Preparing your own meals really takes no longer than sitting in a drive-through or standing in food checkout lines. It's all about being organized and assigning bits of preparation to other family members occasionally.

So, to this day, I enjoy being in the kitchen, more than any other part of the house, testing and honing new ideas, changing up and mixing in the old.

Delicious Duxelles Delight—Mushroom Trinity

Plain and simple, yes. Boring? Absolutely not…

Heat butter in a skillet until it is quite hot but not brown.

Sauté finely chopped onion and shallots, until just barely translucent. Sprinkle with a pinch of dried thyme. Remove from heat and place in a warm dish.

In the same skillet, sauté finely sliced garlic. Lower the heat and watch closely. When the garlic is soft, mash it with a fork. Sprinkle with a little salt and freshly ground pepper and add it to the onions in the waiting dish.

Add more butter to the hot skillet. Increase heat, but be careful not to burn it. Toss finely chopped (not minced) white button mushrooms in the butter to coat.

Sizzle the mushrooms on very high heat, just once over lightly. Quickly sprinkle with a pinch of dried thyme. No salt.

Add it to the waiting warm dish.

Now, deglaze the skillet with your favorite brandy or wine. Reduce the liquid to almost nothing and scrape the skillet drippings into the waiting warm dish.

The mushrooms might start to leak liquid. If cooked swiftly on high heat, this is less likely to happen. Watch closely.

Now add to the hot skillet a quarter cup of half and half cream. Scald, and bring the warming dish contents back to the skillet. Merge all the flavors.

Gently reheat and serve one of several ways: On toast as a midnight treat, or use it as stuffing to make savory profiteroles. It's a beautiful *choux* paste delight.

Or as a delightful tempt-your-taste-buds treat, serve on crispy black olive bread, as tapas.

To indulge your senses further, sprinkle the mushroom trinity with crumbled blue cheese or fresh grated Parmesan.

However, you serve it, sprinkle with homemade fresh crispy bacon bits and a fluttering of fresh chopped parsley and/or fresh basil. (Mint doesn't work.)

A bold red wine such as shiraz goes beautifully with this treat and cleanses the palette.

You will find this charmer on your table often. Guests will rave, and family will indulge in the sensory love from the kitchen as the fragrances permeate the air.

Black Olive Bread—Sprouts and Tapas

Don't ever toss out your leftover favorite black olive bread.

There's some fabulous small bakery olive bread to be had, should you choose not to make your own. But only buy it as you intend to use it or freeze it fresh. It doesn't keep well, particularly in hot humid weather.

Olive bread is wonderful toasted. Or pop it under the broiler briefly to use as the base for tapas.

Some people love to eat the end pieces of any bread; if it's not for you, find a perfect use for those end pieces.

One of my favorite uses for the end pieces is to let them dry out on the counter overnight covered loosely with a fresh clean tea towel.

Break the crusty dried bread into large chunks. Whir quickly in the food processor until you have loose bread crumbs, not fine crumbs. Again, at this stage you can collect the breadcrumbs in your freezer for use on another day.

One such wonderful use: Melt a few tablespoons of butter in a stainless-steel skillet.

Sauté a teaspoon of finely sliced garlic on high heat, but be careful not to burn the butter or the garlic. If you do, there is no salvaging it. Toss it in the trash, wash the skillet and start again.

When the garlic is soft and translucent, mash the garlic with a fork. Remove the garlic bits. Save in a waiting saucer.

Add a little more butter to the skillet. Turn the heat to high but watch it carefully so you don't burn the butter.

When the butter is bubbly and hot, add a cup of the olive bread coarse crumbs. Using an egg-turner type spatula backward, move the breadcrumbs around in the skillet until they start to get just a little bit crispy, not rock hard.

Add back the mashed garlic to the hot toasty olive breadcrumbs and stir to combine.

You will notice that I didn't add salt. The olive bread has enough salt.

Remove the skillet contents to a waiting warm dish.

Add more butter to the empty hot skillet. Add cooked Brussels sprouts that are fork tender. Using the backward egg turner again, keeping the heat high, move the sprouts around in the hot skillet until they brown, saving the browned stuck-on bits.

Some of the outer leaves will separate; that's how it should be. Add back to the skillet. The olive breadcrumb mix and stir into the browned sprouts. It looks a little messy. That's perfect. Remove from heat.

Toast or broil medium thin-sliced olive bread. Drizzle bread with olive oil or a tiny bit of melted butter. Top each slice with a tablespoon of the sprout mixture.

Now for the gourmet topper: Add a half teaspoon of homemade plum jam and a couple of twists of fresh peppercorns. Sprinkle with just a few grains of dried Parmesan cheese.

This might sound like an odd mix, but trust me—it's mega delicious.

Another variable: Add thinly sliced white button mushrooms, seared once over lightly in very hot butter and sprinkled with dry thyme, to the Brussels sprouts mix.

The Brussels sprouts mixture is a fabulous side dish with stovetop sautéed small pork loin. Sliced thinly, serve the pork loin as a tapas; again using the dark olive bread as a base.

Royal Breakfast or Brunch:

"Eggs-ceptional"

Breakfast fit for a king or queen—or to feed your personal president or lord or lady of your castle.

Here's breakfast fit for a king or queen—or to feed your personal president or lord or lady of your castle. Great for Easter, for Father's Day or for no special occasion at all.

Warm a generous patty of frozen herb butter in a stainless-steel skillet until melted. The butter needs to be hot, not browned because browned butter completely changes the taste of anything that comes near it. Because the butter takes on a nutty flavor, be careful not to burn it.

Wilt a very finely chopped generous tablespoon of Spanish onion in your skillet. Add a tablespoon of finely chopped sweet red bell pepper (always cut peppers working from skin side to flesh so as not to have bitter peppers). Add a teaspoon of finely chopped sun-dried tomato; dry or bottled in oil. Sauté for just a minute. You don't want mush. Next, mince a small garlic clove, mashed with lemon and salt. Sauté on medium low heat.

Using a slotted egg turner, return the sautéed mixture to the skillet just to warm through. Then remove to wait in a holding dish.

Fry three rashers of top-grade fatty bacon in the same skillet until medium crispy and set aside. When frying bacon, do not turn the bacon rashers or move them around; just leave them alone. Resist the urge to touch. Just before removing them from the pan, turn the rashers just briefly and finish up the frying on the other side. That's the very best way to fry bacon. You are not making crumbled bacon.

Add a little more butter to the pan with the bacon fat drippings. Sauté four firm, medium-size chopped white button mushrooms, again on high heat but you don't want crispy mushrooms. Sprinkle with a pinch of dried thyme. No salt (it makes the mushrooms weep). Sprinkle with dry thyme.

Do not overcook the mushrooms; just sear them. Just turn once over lightly (you don't want mushy mushrooms) and remove the mushrooms from the skillet and save with peppers and onion mix.

Add more butter to the skillet and sauté a half dozen medium-size shrimp. Sprinkle the shrimp with dry thyme.

When the shrimp is no longer translucent, it's cooked. Remove from heat immediately. Like everything else, the shrimp continues to cook in its own heat. So be very careful not to overcook. The shrimp will get rubbery.

If you have cooked the shrimp with the shells on, now remove the shells.

Deglaze the skillet with your favorite brandy. Scrape the pan clean using an egg turner. Add the drippings to the onion mix.

In a separate or clean skillet, melt a couple of tablespoons of plain butter. You are going to cook scrambled eggs in this clean skillet. You don't want any crunchy bits in the pan.

Just eggs. Nothing added. No water; no milk or cream. No spices, either.

Whisk six whole large eggs in a bowl. Just incorporate a little air. Gently drop the whisked eggs into the hot butter and start to move the eggs around the pan immediately as they congeal. Don't leave the stove. Keep heat medium high. You don't want the eggs to stick to the pan.

Do not let the eggs brown. I rarely use a Teflon coated pan in any way shape or form. And I highly recommend using a copper bottom stainless steel skillet for all my recipes. A skillet has low sides. Invest in a glass top cover, so you can see what's going on while you cook. If you don't currently use a good skillet, I recommend investing in one. Good ones last for 20 years or more if taken care of. And for making the scrambled eggs, at their very best, this works like a charm. You might be surprised.

Using an egg turner backward, lift and continuously move the eggs, until just barely cooked. They should look moist. Always remember, food continues to cook when removed from the heat source. You don't want to make an omelet. It is very important to keep moving the eggs continuously as they cook, mounding the eggs gently. This will only take a minute or two.

This egg consistency is just beautiful to see and wonderful to eat. They are pure eggs. Do not overcook. That would change the taste of the eggs completely.

Transfer the eggs, evenly divided, into two oven-to-table flat low serving dishes. I like to use oval midsize, low-sided, oven-proof ramekins.

Sprinkle with a little salt, a few twists of course ground black pepper and a dusting of fine paprika powder.

Divide the onion, bell pepper and garlic mix over top the loosely scrambled eggs. Don't stir.

Now the bit that makes this dish extra special. Split six pimento stuffed green Manzanilla olives (McLaren's brand is by far the best but often very difficult to find) in half, top to bottom, and position around the edge of the beautiful eggs. Sprinkle each dish with a few drops of the olive jar liquid.

I know some people don't care for olives, but truly this makes the egg dish spectacular. Do try it because all that happens is the flavors burst in your mouth, combined.

Position the cooked whole shrimp around the outside edge of each dish. Precooked, thawed whole medium size frozen shrimp will do in a pinch, if you don't have fresh; but fresh is noticeably better.

Divide the bacon strips and position on top of the eggs. Now for the grand finish. Top each serving dish with a large slice of cheddar cheese. Cheddar works best with this dish.

But, absolutely necessary: Sprinkle the cheese slice with grated rock-hard strong Parmesan cheese (perfect use for a leftover hard bit) and a sprinkle of very dry Romano. (These two cheeses marry wonderfully well.) A few twists of black pepper and you're done.

Place both serving dishes on a cookie sheet, under preheated broiler on the top rack with the oven door open, just until the cheese bubbles. Just seconds. You don't want the cheese to brown.

Serve with toast triangles. No need for another meal till dinnertime. A brunch glass of dry white wine acts as a great palate cleanser. Enjoy.

No one will ever be disappointed with this 'adult' breakfast dish.

To broaden your breakfast experience, making it into a brunch meal, just serve a side salad of tomatoes, such as this recipe: Salad on the Run—Instant Fresh Tomato Basil Salad…(We eat first with our eyes)

Whole Salmon—Poached in Winzertanz

Two delicious salmon recipes for you to try.

In the early 1980s, a dear friend from England, who didn't cook, asked if she and her husband went to the St. Lawrence Market and got a whole salmon, would I prepare it for them. I was delighted she asked.

I can't remember the occasion, but it turned out to be a great party. We were a group of mixed cultures and got to share various food offerings at functions. It was a wonderful food learning experience as each couple had a different nationality and prepared their native foods: Jamaican, Barbados and other Caribbean guests; Croatia, South African, Indian, German and English.

For that event, aside from preparing the whole poached salmon, I prepared my own St. Jacques Coquille on the half shell. It was a big job for feeding a large group but there was enough for each. Transporting is always a challenge.

Here is my own personal recipe for whole oven poached salmon in Winzertanz. This was about a 6–7-pound salmon.

Poach the whole salmon, head and tail on. Ideally have the fishmonger descale it. Rinse in very cold water. Sprinkle the fish inside and out with salt and a little pepper.

Line the poaching pan with a large piece of cheesecloth, generously draping it over the sides.

In the perfect size poaching pan (you can use just a tinfoil turkey roasting pan in a pinch), I put the cleaned whole fish. I covered the fish completely with mild chicken broth (only use homemade) and added a bay leaf, a couple of stalks each of fresh carrots, celery, a quartered white Spanish onion, a sprig of dill, a couple of whole cloves and a few capers.

Add salt, fresh ground peppercorns, a pinch of thyme and two quartered lemons. Then the most important: Four to six cups of Winzertanz depending on the size of the fish.

Place the poaching pan on a foil oven liner pan to catch any drips. Keep the oven clean. Cover the poaching pan with its lid, or close completely using foil, shiny side in. Poke a steam vent hole.

In a preheated oven set at 350–375 F, position the fish pan midway top to bottom, side to side. Reduce heat immediately to 325 F. Keep the oven door closed. No peeking. Allow about 7–10 minutes per inch thickness. You want the salmon to be just done.

Using the cheesecloth as handles, remove the fish from the poaching liquid and place the hot fish on to a cheesecloth-lined baking sheet with sides. Let it rest. When able to handle it, slip off the skin.

When the broth is cooled just slightly, pour it into a large stainless-steel pot. Bring to a soft boil for a few minutes, then strain through cheesecloth in a sieve.

Clarify using egg shells so that you have a fish consommé. Add finely minced red bell pepper, minced green onion and just a pinch of crushed garlic.

Next: Stir in gelatin packets as per product suggestion.

Pour the broth into a loaf pan to set. Then cut in cubes to surround the cooled fish on a decorated serving platter. Or pour gelatin broth into cold shot glasses, to act as a mold, and when just starting to set, add a party Popsicle stick.

Note: An alternate for another day: Make broth Popsicle stick molds adding chopped (only) lobster claw meat. It's a really special treat. The saved shells from seafood makes great broth in the same fashion.

For decorating the whole salmon, make firm tomato roses and lemon curls, and/or pretty mimosa half-stuffed eggs.

As a side, serve my multicolored cherry tomato salad.

http://www.remonline.com/recipes-busy-sales-reps-spectacular-barbecue-serving-sauce/

My German potato salad and my incredible homemade dill bread finish the feast.

This is a great buffet treat for any special occasion.

Painted Salmon

Here's another suggestion. Visit your fishmonger and ask him to give you a fresh, never frozen salmon center cut from behind the gills. Have him scrape the scales for you. He will likely have a boning knife that is razor sharp, much sharper than yours.

A super sharp knife does a much faster, easier and better scaling job. If you are scaling yourself, be absolutely certain to always position the knife so it is moving away from you.

Never buy salmon that is wrapped in a prepackaged plastic wrap on the fish counter at your grocery store. Believe it or not, it could have been re-packed, with a new best before date.

When you take your salmon home, refrigerate it immediately, keeping it in its paper wrapping. Don't open the package until you are ready to prepare the salmon.

Rinse delicately in very cold water. Pat dry. Leave the skin on, but remove the skin when the salmon is cooked.

Spritz the salmon with Asbach or your favorite brandy.

Paint with a mixture of mustard and maple syrup, equal parts. Sprinkle with salt and fresh ground pepper. Drizzle with brandy fig *jus* from your marinating jar.

Toss a few capers into the package. Lay a whole paper, thin slice of onion on top of the salmon skin and a slice of lemon. Position a sprig of dill on top. Close the package with a double roll seam.

Make a papillote using two layers of parchment paper; overlap and fold a seam if the paper is not large enough. Poke a couple of tiny air holes in the package using the tip of a sharp knife.

Using a preheated, very hot barbecue grill, turn off all the burners. Position your papillote on a metal barbecue grate sheet with holes. A flat barbecue vegetable grill pan will do.

Turn off the barbecue. Close the lid tight. Guesstimate timing: Allow 5 minutes per inch of thickness.

Remove from heat and let it sit just briefly. Remember the fish will continue to steam in its package. Do not overcook. The salmon needs to be just done.

Leave the salmon in its papillote, using a sharp knife to open the package. Be careful. The package is full of very hot steam. Position the papillote on a bed of shredded lettuce, surrounded by lemon wedges.

Serve with my homemade potato salad, fresh asparagus, and a squeeze of fresh lemon.

Homemade ice cream drizzled with an Asbach brandy reduced figgy sauce is an ideal way to finish up this light delicious meal.

'Just' A Hamburger—But, Extraordinaire—And My Blender Salad Dressing

When you bite into the meat, the flavor of the cognac marinated fig will release along with the gooey blue cheese. It's a wonderful, adult gourmet treat.

Using a pound of never frozen medium ground beef, mix in your favorite herbs. I mostly use just a little dried thyme and a pinch of garlic salt.

Work in a whisked whole egg. Stir in two tablespoons of figgy jus from your Asbach Uralt black mission fig cognac marinating jar. Add salt and pepper. Let rest in fridge for a half hour.

Shape into generous hamburgers. Chop a small macerated marinated fig in half and insert the fig in a hole in the center of each hamburger. In the same hole, poke a piece of fridge-hard blue cheese. Wrap the hamburger around the indent, reshaping it to enclose the fig and cheese. Don't compact the meat too firmly, just enough so it keeps its shape on the grill.

Refrigerate until it's ready to grill. Oil the grill so the meat doesn't stick. Rub the meat patties with a little oil. Don't make the grill too hot and turn only once. Keep the grill on medium heat. Do not overcook the hamburgers. Remove from the grill and tent to allow to rest so juices redistribute.

Serve on your favorite hamburger bun with crispy fresh iceberg lettuce, a fat slice of fresh tomato, a generous fresh basil leaf and if you like, a slice of crispy bacon. No pickles, ketchup or relish on this burger. No additional accompaniments.

When you bite into the meat the flavor of the cognac marinated fig will release along with the gooey blue cheese. It's a wonderful, adult gourmet treat.

If you don't like blue cheese, substitute a tiny piece of cold Brie or Camembert.

Now for Something Really Different

Wash whole beefsteak tomatoes and cut the tops off about 10 percent from the size. Hollow out the whole tomato. Save the innards, minus seeds.

Crumble or chop the grilled hamburger quite fine. Chop the tomato's innards and flesh. Mince a small piece of shallot and mash and mince a small piece of garlic clove. Stir well. Chop and add an artichoke heart from a jar, packed in oil.

Mix the crumpled hamburger with little homemade coarse, fresh seasoned breadcrumbs as a binder. Chop fresh basil chiffonade, tarragon and mint leaves, and chop Italian parsley. Add to the mix.

Spray the inside of the firm fresh tomatoes with just a little olive oil. Sprinkle salt and pepper inside.

Spoon the filling into hollow beefsteak tomatoes. Add a few breadcrumbs on top and a little dry Parmesan cheese. Replace the tomato tops, as covers. Using a square baking pan with sides, bake the stuffed whole tomatoes at 325 F for about 20–25 minutes.

Remove from the oven and drizzle with reduced white balsamic vinegar, to which you have added a little figgy *jus* from your cognac marinating jar. Spritz the outside of baked stuffed tomatoes with olive oil.

Serve in a feta cheese puddle: Purée cheese with a little cream and a little ice water. Mince a little cucumber and mix into the cheese sauce. Stir in a little cracked pepper and a pinch of salt.

Now

If a salad suits your fancy, a mix of various lettuces, halved hard cooked eggs and several of your favorite raw veggies, dressed for dinner in one of my finest salad dressings, should be an earthmoving plate, completed. Wonderful fragrances.

In the mid-80s, one day, as I was preparing dinner, I realized I had collected lots of bits and pieces of still-fresh produce in the crisper in the fridge. By the way, bits and pieces of bell peppers, seeds in, and even onion, cut side down, saved on a small bed of live fresh basil leaves, will keep for ages in the fridge, on an open plate.

Being one not to waste, and in the mood for a very fresh salad dressing, I just started adding things to the blender. Here's the extremely yummy result:

My Special Blender Salad Dressing, Or Dip

In blender:

2 tablespoons peeled and pitted; chopped cucumber

1/3 small, very fresh, garlic clove (more later)

½ teaspoon salt

¼ teaspoon fresh ground pepper

2 tablespoon vinegar

¼ teaspoon French's regular mustard

1 raw egg yolk

1 whole raw egg

1 small whole clove of garlic

1 tiny piece of white onion

1 small piece of red pepper, skin on

1 tiny piece of green pepper, skin on

1 tablespoon Romano dry Kraft grated cheese (for some reason the fresh Romano doesn't work)

1 tablespoon fresh dill (or dried)

1 teaspoon dried thyme leaves (not the ground thyme)

A tiny sprinkle of dried mint

4 olives (Manzanilla green olives, pimento stuffed)

1 tablespoon of liquid from a jar of pimento stuff green olives (McLaren's is best brand)

1 small, chopped, artichoke from jar packed in oil

1 tablespoon full fat sour cream

Turn on the blender and one by one add and swirl the ingredients in the blender, running at high speed. Leave the blender running and through the fine hole, add Mazola Corn Oil, very gradually at first, until you use up to 1–1/2 cups of oil.

The texture will be like a thick but runny mayonnaise. Stir in juice of just a small slice of fresh lemon. And a teaspoon of lemon zest.

Store in a covered, airtight, glass container or screw-top glass jar, in fridge. Never store anything that has vinegar or citrus in it in plastic. It keeps for several days.

Use as a general salad dressing or as a dip for crudités.

No one will not enjoy this, even people who claim they don't like salads or raw vegetables.

In addition: My Ever so Fresh Salad: One of my all-time favorites…

One medium-large head of iceberg lettuce

Small head of hydroponic leaf lettuce (Boston Bibb)

Very small head of Romaine lettuce

Small red radicchio

Chop coarsely, a cup of fresh, firm, white button mushrooms

Chopped, fresh, seeded tomatoes. Skin on, red and green

Halved hard-cooked eggs; however many you enjoy

Half-head of celery (top half, including leaves); chopped

Green bell pepper pieces

Red bell pepper pieces

Yellow bell pepper pieces

Salt and pepper (fresh ground)

Wash sand out of the lettuce, using hot water, very carefully, and shake dry in a clean dish-drying towel. Rewrap, tightly, in a fresh towel and put in the bottom, coldest part of the fridge. It will get crispy like just picked from your garden.

Drain a can of chick peas (garbanzo beans) and sprinkle with thyme. Mince a tiny piece of onion.

Toss everything together with mixed lettuce pieces, and there you have it. Serve in a beautiful, wooden salad bowl.

Serve salad dressing in a glass bowl with a small soup or gravy ladle at the table, and everyone can add their own dressing to their crisp, fresh, salad plate.

Enjoy! Bring summer to your table all year long.

Stuffed Green Bell Peppers

People sometimes say they don't have time to cook. It's one thing if you simply don't like cooking, but if you do and think you can't fit it into your schedule, it's no different than other types of time management.

I was in my mid-20s. I made this recipe for Sunday guests, thinking two generous size green bell peppers, stuffed, for each would be sufficient. I learned a valuable lesson that day and received nice compliments. The biggest one: Next time be sure to make more.

Cautiously, to be polite, Poppa A asked for seconds; someone who would never do that in someone else's home. I was completely honored. A nice memory from the one who insisted that I must eat Brussels sprouts and creamed endive in béchamel sauce (that I had never heard of), complete with fresh grated nutmeg. That was more than 50 years ago.

So many recipes start this way. Buy fresh (never frozen —it tastes different, as does most meat) medium fat ground beef.

Brown the beef well but you don't want it to be crunchy. It is very important to the final taste that the beef is browned sufficiently. Finely chop an onion and add to the meat. Add a small handful of finely chopped firm white button mushrooms. Sprinkle salt and pepper.

Cover the pot to "sweat" the onions. Stay at the stove. Add a clove of garlic. Don't cut the garlic or smash it.

You want the delicate garlic flavor to enhance all the other ingredients. Mash the garlic with a fork when it is fork tender. Add a large tin of whole tomatoes and sauce. Using a fork, break up the tomatoes. Heat and stir to combine flavors.

Add an equal portion of cooked, steamed, plain white rice that is just barely cooked. Stir all the ingredients together and set aside. Allow the flavors to marry.

Now, back then, I didn't know much about cooking with herbs and spices so it was simple; I didn't use any.

Wash a dozen green peppers. Chop the tops off about an inch down from the top, keeping the "handle" in place. Scoop out seeds and using a spoon, remove some of the fibrous tissue.

Bring a large pot of salted water to a roaring boil. Lid on. If the peppers look like they might not want to stand upright, slice a tiny bit off the bottom, before par boiling, to stabilize. Not much.

Using tongs, insert the peppers into the boiling water, reduce heat and par boil the peppers. No lid. Don't walk away from the stove. This just takes a couple of minutes. The peppers are not cooked. This procedure will help preserve the bright green color if done properly.

Using tongs, remove the par boiled whole peppers and drain on a rack over a cookie sheet.

Fill each pepper to capacity with the meat and rice filling. Push the filling down a little bit, but not hard. You don't want to crack the peppers.

Position the stuffed peppers, touching one another, upright in a roasting pan, with the pepper lids in place.

Tent with tinfoil, shiny side in. Bake in the preheated oven at 350 F until the skin on the peppers can easily be pierced. You don't want the peppers to get mushy. Likely, 20 minutes will be enough baking time. But quickly close the oven door; you don't want the heat to escape to lower the oven temperature.

Always remember, food continues to cook in its own heat once removed from the oven.

While the peppers bake, heat your favorite plain, bottled, tomato sauce; homemade or store bought. Add a bay leaf or two to the sauce. Don't boil but make sure the sauce is very hot, because it cools quickly.

Place two stuffed green peppers with lids in place, on each serving plate, in a puddle of hot tomato sauce. Serve extra sauce in a gravy boat. Sprinkle finely grated dry Parmesan cheese on each plate as you serve. Some people like a dollop of sour cream on top, sprinkled with mild Hungarian paprika. That's my personal favorite.

Keep the remaining peppers warm in the turned off oven, with the door ajar.

Although these stuffed green bell peppers are filling, many will want seconds. If you have leftovers, they reheat well and a fresh drizzle of tomato sauce will make them seem fresh all over again. They do not freeze well after they are baked, but if you insist, freeze them after they are stuffed but before they are baked. Then bake frozen.

Perhaps take leftovers to work. Only microwave for a few seconds. Split them in half or quarters before reheating. It helps speed up the reheat process.

If you are participating in a pot luck supper, or are invited to bring a dish to someone else's house, make a large amount in an oversize turkey roasting pan. Reheat when you get there. Serve and enjoy.

Everyone will want the recipe.

Many recipes go back to the 70s when life was so much simpler. And gourmet certainly wasn't what it is today. I don't make esoteric things, as many gourmet folks do. Just good, basic home cooking, dressed for company, or to enjoy at home, on the road, or even at a picnic, or to take along to someone else's place. Even occasionally for gift giving.

People sometimes say they don't have time to cook. It's one thing if you simply don't like cooking, but if you do and think you can't fit it into your schedule, it's no different than other types of time management.

I never worked less than a 60-hour week in my four-decade real estate career and in busy markets, I put in even more hours. Every day, I arranged my schedule to be home to cook dinner. The only way that can work is if you are super organized, using schedules and calendars. And you must schedule in "me-time" just for you, even if it's just tub-time.

It's only in really recent years we've had smart phones and computers to help us be organized. Shop in off hours; I can't bear to stand in line-ups. It's not always practical to shop in large stores. Parking and push and shove shopping environments are exhausting. And you don't always save shopping in large bulk with no place to store it all at home.

Shop in medium-large stores, mostly only buy sale items; you will get to know the best prices. Choose a maximum of three regular store brands, ideally near one another. Ideally just two, and a third for emergency finds.

Time wasted running all over town, gas wasted and comparison shopping can take way too much time and energy. Once in a while, splurge and stock up; but don't do that kind of shopping every week. Make lists. Always add an item to your watch-for list, when you break out the last bottle or container. That way, you will never run out of things like deodorant and toilet tissue, laundry soap, toothpaste and such.

I know people who don't stock up on bacon, for example, because they rarely eat it. But when they do, they really enjoy it. Bacon freezes wonderfully well. Cut the package in half crosswise. Freeze half until you need a bacon fix. That's just one example.

Preparing a recipe book is a time-consuming process. Making recipes, when you love to cook, is a joy. But the record-keeping and typing out of each one, and editing and keeping track is a massive undertaking. But for me, it's my joy and entertainment; still my hobby after all the years.

So far, a couple of years' time and my manuscript keeps growing. I can only eat so much, and people seem to love my original recipes. Hindsight is always foresight. Although I saved all my recipes and gourmet newspaper columns, and other writings I saved over the years, I wish I had prepared the cookbook years ago.

Pommes Frites (The Real Thing)

Here's my recipe from the 1970s—it's ageless.

I fry in corn oil; Mazola Oil is cholesterol free. Heat the oil at a medium heat, 325 degrees. Use a heavy coated cast iron pot. Never use a lightweight pot when deep frying—it's way too dangerous!

Invest in a thermometer suitable for deep fryer use. You never want the oil to boil. Never fill the pot more than halfway with oil and always deep fry in small quantities. Never turn your back or multitask when deep frying.

Have plenty of paper towels on hand and clean, dry, tossable cloth dish towels. You'll need a container to dispose of the used oil properly. Never pour it down the sink.

Wash all containers completely in very hot soapy water before putting them in your dishwasher. Otherwise, the oil will clog up the dishwasher.

Soak whole peeled, medium large, firm potatoes in a sugar, salt-and-cold-water mix for a half hour. Just a couple of tablespoons of sugar and half as much salt with a few cups of cold water. Let stand, covered, on the counter.

Cut the potatoes lengthwise into medium large size fries.

Pat them dry with a clean tea towel but do not rinse. You want to keep the starch.

Deep fry the medium-large fries for about five minutes at 325 F. Control the temperature closely. They won't be cooked. Drain the fries in a metal colander on the paper towel. Remember: They are not cooked.

Wrap the fries in a clean tea towel that you can later toss in the trash. Put the wrapped fries in the coldest part of the fridge on a metal cookie sheet for about an hour.

Remove the oil from the heat source while the fries are in the fridge. Cover the pot. Wipe up any splatters. Keep work surface spotless, not just for safety.

Keep the fries wrapped and cold. Bring the oil pot back to the burner. Uncover the pot before reheating the oil. Allow the oil to reach 400 degrees, pot uncovered. Never put a lid on an oil pot while in use on a burner.

Unwrap the cold fries and carefully, using a large slotted spoon, gently lower the cold fries into the very hot oil. Just a few at a time as the 400-degree oil will drop temperature very quickly.

The potatoes will "poof"…and you have pommes frites; the most wonderful "French" fries ever. Salt while still super-hot. Dipping sauce, if you enjoy it, can be aioli, made any way you like it, or homemade tomato ketchup or sour cream sauce. Whatever suits your fancy. Some people enjoy a flurry shower of granular sugar on their frites.

I made frites for the first time in the mid-1970s. It initially took a bit of careful doing to keep the oil at a just-right controlled temperature. It's much easier to control using a gas fire than electric, but doable. But monitoring the oil temperature is most important, because the very cold fries drop the oil temperature rapidly.

Note: Fry in small batches and keep adjusting the fire under the oil pot. Enjoy! Best fries ever! These pommes frites are a nice accompaniment to many dishes, and work especially well as a side dish to any of my recipes at my sea food birthday party fare grouping.

Check here:

http://www.remonline.com/seafood-supreme-sole-shrimp-sea-scallops-and-more /
Note: If you barbecue outside on a patio (I don't recommend this for balcony preparation) and are lucky enough to have an add-on, additional freestanding attached burner, this recipe can be made outside and is a wonderful treat with your favorite barbecued steak and fresh salad. Perhaps this is a good choice:

http://www.remonline.com/gourmet-cooking-for-real-estate-professionals-salad-on-the-run/

How to make friends (or enemies) with your neighbors: When the fragrances of your meal-making efforts waft through the air, you might hear from them. And this is a recipe you will want to make at the cottage, but I can't stress often enough, when deep frying be careful and dispose properly anything with oil attached and the oil itself. Do not reuse deep frying oil. What you save in the cost of buying new oil, is not worth doing.

Figgy Stuffed Pork Chop (Or Chicken Breast)

Plus, it's a "figgy" thing—**Butterscotch Figgy Sauce.**

Mix a cup of chopped Asbach brandy-marinated black mission figs with little fresh coarse homemade breadcrumbs (sautéed in real butter), minced shallots and a sprinkle of crushed fresh thyme. Add a dollop of my tomato butter. Remove from heat. Stir in just a drop of roasted garlic purée and a little mustard. Salt and fresh ground pepper. Refrigerate until you are ready to stuff thick center cut pork chops.

Using a very sharp boning knife, slit each uncooked pork chop to make a deep pocket that will accept the stuffing. Careful not to cut all the way through.

Note: Marinate the pork chops in a sealed glass dish; turn once. Use your favorite marinade, or use my bell pepper marinade:

http://www.remonline.com/gourmet-recipes-real-estate-professionals-pepper-marinade/

Let the pork chops marinade for a couple of hours in the fridge. Never leave pork or poultry on the counter in hot humid weather.

Speaking of poultry: You can cut a slit pocket in a generous size bone-in skinless chicken breast, as an alternate use for this stuffing. Follow the same recipe procedure.

Lift out the pork chops using tong and pat dry. Insert a tablespoon of the cold stuffing into each slit.

Line a barbecue grill pan with foil, shiny side in, against the pan. Place two large double layers of foil on the counter, shiny side to shiny side, large enough so the pork chops can lay positioned on the foil not overlapping. Cover with another double layer of foil, shiny to shiny side, and fold the edges to make a package, to catch juices. Lay the chops on the foiled grill pan. Prick the foil in a few spots to let steam escape.

Preheat the barbecue to very hot. Turn it off and place the pork chop grill pan on the grates. Close the barbecue lid. When the juices run clear the chops are ready to eat. Timing will depend on the thickness and size of the chops. Likely, 15 minutes should work. Remove the foil package of chops from the barbecue and let rest at least five minutes before serving, so juices redistribute.

Serve with favorite grilled potatoes papillote and grilled veggies. Bonus: Inhale the fragrant goodness treat. Mop up any juices with a grilled crostini smeared with a little roasted garlic puree.

This recipe is also wonderful if you use boned chicken breast.

It's A "Figgy" Thing ~ Butterscotch Figgy Sauce

Melt half a pound of unsalted butter in a stainless-steel pot, on medium heat. Add two cups of golden-brown sugar. Stir with a wooden spoon. Let the butter sugar mix come to a bubble. Stop. Be careful, because the mixture will turn rock hard. Turn off the heat immediately. Let stand for five minutes.

On low heat, stir in a half cup of Asbach brandy black mission fig thick marinating jus. Replace the brandy in the jar each time you use jus, and keep adding a supply of figs. You will find so many uses for them.

Stir into the pot a half cup of cold liquid whipping cream until fully incorporated. Add just a sprinkle of salt. Drop a quarter stick of real butter into the pot. The butter is not meant to incorporate completely; it's just meant to make the sauce shiny. Just give a gentle stir. Remove from heat. Cool to room temperature.

Store it in the fridge in a covered mason jar. Cover the jar first with two layers of wax paper. When ready to serve, gently reheat the sauce in a bain-marie, or just bring to room temperature. Whisk a little sauce in a dish. Turn into a mini gravy boat.

Use as a caramel sauce on homemade vanilla ice cream, served in a champagne flute, with a delicate long-handled fruit spoon. Top the glass with a halved fresh black mission fig or use the figgy butterscotch sauce as a drizzle over a cheesecake that you have topped with a couple of brandy marinated, but not macerated, black mission figs. They should be interspersed with seared fresh figs, cut in half and seared flesh side, once over only in very hot butter. Not cooked, just seared, or you can sear the flesh side with a portable flame. Sprinkle the seared fresh figs with coarse sugar. If there is any butter left in the skillet, use a rubber spatula and drain into the butterscotch jar.

OR: Scald a cup of cream in the leftover figgy butter drippings, let reduce a little, mash a couple of macerated figs from your jar into the cream, and serve the thickened cream over a small dish of brandy marinated figs, alongside a half-inch slice of fresh homemade pound cake, served with a smear of crème Anglaise. Or during the Christmas holidays, serve the figgy cream alongside a generous slice of my Asbach Stollen.

http://www.remonline.com/getting-ahead-of-the-holiday-season/

Serve individual, plain New York cheesecake slices on a lace doily on an oversize see-through glass plate, centered on a large charger, alongside a few fresh basil leaves, just picked, and maybe add a few dipped "ground cherries." Drizzle the butterscotch figgy sauce over the cheesecake. Position a cake fork at an angle on the glass plate.

OR: Dip into the butterscotch figgy sauce, a few "ground cherries," also known as Cape Gooseberries. Remove the paper-like husk that is similar to the covering on a tomatillo and pop one of these gooseberries into your mouth, for a fruit delicacy. Dip the berries in the sauce and drop on top of a serving of zabaglione, topped with a dollop of Chantilly cream, and drizzle on a little sauce. Probably like nothing you have enjoyed before.

And, another dessert idea: Make panna cotta with finely chopped fresh basil. Top with a drizzle of the butterscotch sauce, or even the figgy cream.

It's a nice dessert whichever way you choose to use the figgy butterscotch sauce.

Alternate—A Savory Idea:

Make my Lazy Sole recipe.

[Scroll down; it's in the comments at:]

http://www.remonline.com/seafood-supreme-sole-shrimp-sea-scallops-and-more/

Drizzle just a tiny bit of warm, figgy butterscotch sauce over one end of the fish, just as you are ready to serve. Top the drizzle with a little fresh ground peppercorn. Add a handful of fresh basil leaves to the platter. The Lazy Sole will love you. So will your guests.

And another use for the figgy scalded cream: Drizzle a little over my fig stuffed center cut pork chop, or on a fig stuffed chicken breast. Beyond yum.

Bay Scallop Basil (Silver Dollar-Size) Blintz Treat

This is a wonderful addition to any indoor buffet table.

I mostly don't use a recipe and sometimes don't write things down when I should. But I decided this was definitely worth sharing in my cookbook.

I wanted to try "scallop" baby blintzes. The store did not have sea scallops, so I bought a cup (way too much) of little bay scallops. I don't like bay scallops ordinarily; they are quite sweet—I prefer the big sea scallops. But I figured for making the blintzes, the bay scallops should work fine. Did I say fine? The result is definitely a keeper. You will love this recipe.

Typically, I just do the big sea scallops once over lightly in butter, a tiny pinch of salt and pepper and a little pinch of dried thyme (not the powder bottled thyme). Whatever you do, never overcook scallops. They will be like bouncing rubber balls: Inedible. In any season, they are expensive; sometimes outrageously so. Be very careful when buying scallops. Sometimes the stores freeze their supply and thaw them and sell as fresh. Know your fish counter people. Off scallops can make you very ill. Demand to know that they are fresh.

For the blintzes, I put the cup of bay scallops (drained, but not rinsed) in the blender (not in a food processor), added about a teaspoon of fresh basil, a pinch of salt and pepper, a pinch of dry fresh thyme leaves (you can add any herb you like I think—maybe even dill would work—or just parsley or green onion maybe). Or a mix of all of them. Whatever makes your taste buds happy.

Don't whiz for long—just a minute to crush the scallops to a mush. Perhaps, depending on your blender, pulse just a couple of times. Add a couple of tablespoons of ordinary flour. Not much. Half the flour if you use half the amount of scallops. Add 1/8 cup of cream. I use half and half (coffee cream), less if doing half the recipe. We don't want the mixture to be too runny—sort of like pancake batter.

I heat the butter in the stainless-steel skillet, quite hot but not nutty brown, with just enough butter to cover the pan. Replenish the butter as you fill the pan with additional blintz batter. I scoop a large tablespoon (because you want tiny blintzes) of the mixture into the hot butter, so they cook like large silver dollar coins. When the edge crinkles a little bit, flip them over one by one to just barely cook the other side. Do not overcook. They will continue cooking in their own heat after you remove them from the skillet. Stack them on a paper towel and pat the top side with another sheet of paper towel and arrange on a serving plate. Or, you could serve these baby blintzes hot, just with a dab of my "figgy butter."

Top it with sour cream and/or fresh lox, or anything else you like to taste with the fish family.

Oh, my! I had about 30 or 40 tiny blintzes—no kidding! Way too many. So, another time I would just do a half cup of the bay scallops, if just for me. But they were just impossibly good!

You can serve these scallop basil blintzes at room temperature for guests. This is a wonderful addition to any indoor buffet table and guests can choose how to top their blintz plate.

I don't recommend that you serve these scallop blintzes outside on the patio in hot humid weather.

Serve the baby blintzes, overlapped, on a large platter, surrounded by a collection of large fresh basil leaves; or if you have already added toppings, keep each blintz lying flat, not touching one another, on a large decorative tray.

A fluted champagne glass with crackling rose Royal de Neuville is a remarkable and memorable accompaniment. Remember this recipe for a nice New Year's treat, too.

Faux Blini Coins: Use up Those Leftovers

Don't toss those leftover mashed potatoes. These blini are not potato pancakes, as such, but a wonderful breakfast or brunch treat nonetheless.

You can make blini quickly and easily from fresh parboiled riced potatoes, but this is just a great way not to waste leftovers.

Don't toss those leftover mashed potatoes. These blini are not potato pancakes, as such, but a wonderful breakfast or brunch treat nonetheless.

This will make 20 two-inch blini. For using up two cups of mashed potatoes, stir in about four tablespoons of flour and one whisked whole egg.

Sprinkle with a little garlic salt, lots of wonderful pepper, crushed dry thyme and any other herb that you enjoy. Stir well to combine.

You could add a tablespoon of Kraft grated dry Parmesan cheese or Romano, for a different taste.

In a hot skillet, put a little Mazola corn oil and a little butter. Just a little; you don't want to saturate the blini.

Watch the pan carefully and adjust the heat constantly. Lift the skillet off the burner completely as necessary, while the heat element adjusts. You don't want to burn the potato mix, or even have it too dark-colored. Just a perfect golden color.

Drop large tablespoons of the potato mix into the hot skillet. You want the skillet hot while not browning the oil and butter. When the edges of the potato coins show a little light brown on the underside edge, it's time to turn the blini.

Stack these mini tater blinis on a warm plate. If you want to eat them for breakfast or brunch right away, prepare a fried egg, in a medium hot skillet, in butter, once over lightly. You want the yolk to be cooked but still runny, with no brown edges on the egg white. Slide the gently fried egg over a warm plate of three potato coin blini.

Serve with crispy bacon on the side. Maybe add a slice of cheddar cheese on the blini, first, and serve with a thick slice of beefsteak tomato. Complement with a peppery fresh basil leaf from your herb pot.

It's the easiest gourmet breakfast or brunch ever. And no waste. Nothing goes to waste in my kitchen.

These faux blini are also a special walk-about buffet treat: Serve the faux blini at room temperature with a dollop of sour cream and a twist of smoked salmon slices, on individual little amuse bouche toss-away plates. Sprinkle with a little fresh, chopped dill.

The faux blini can be made using any mashed root veggie: Carrots, turnip, parsnip, kohlrabi. This is a way to get people who don't eat vegetables to partake. They will ask for seconds.

If you have made the Dutch dish as a Stamppot (carrots, onions and potatoes mashed together), you can make leftover blini using this mix in the same way. *Stamppot boerenkool* works, too. A tiny drizzle of vinegar is a must as it enhances the flavor of the kale mix.

There's no end to the combinations you can make: Stir sautéed in butter, finely chopped onions. Or: Chop a fine chiffonade of fresh basil and fold into the leftover mashed potatoes. Or: Chop small chunks of hard cheddar cheese and fold into the potatoes. Got leftover butter-sugar carrots? Chop them fine and fold into the mix. Any root vegetable leftover can be incorporated.

White Truffle Mustard Sautéed Chicken

A song of gladness ~ rhapsody in white truffle mustard sautéed chicken

Marinate a cubed large boneless skinless chicken breast in Mazola Corn Oil for about 10 minutes. Sprinkle with crushed dry fresh thyme leaves. Do not salt, but add lots of fresh ground pepper. A little nutmeg goes a long way, but a quarter teaspoon fluttered over the chicken pieces adds a wonderful touch.

Just before you are ready to sauté, sprinkle with a little garlic salt and a generous amount of regular salt. Toss in the marinating oil.

Using a rubber spatula, wipe the marinating plate clean as you usher the chicken pieces into a very hot sauté skillet with low sides, using all the marinating oil.

Listen for the sizzle. The skillet needs to be very hot, but adjust it so the chicken doesn't burn. Don't touch for a few minutes as the chicken pieces sear. When they don't stick to the pan surface, using an egg turner, move the chicken pieces around the skillet, tumbling them so all sides come in contact with the pan.

This all happens in just minutes like with a minute-steak and the chicken pieces cook very quickly. Don't leave the stove. Remember, always, the chicken will continue to cook in its own heat, so you want it just barely cooked.

Empty the skillet that has a slightly browned surface and add a large dollop of butter. Toss quartered, white button mushrooms (I used about two cups) just to sear once over lightly in the very hot sizzling golden but not brown butter (you don't want *beurre noisette*). Add a half teaspoon of crushed thyme and stir. Add lots of salt and fresh ground pepper, only after the mushrooms have seared. Salt makes mushrooms weep. Wait until they are cooked.

Add the mushrooms to the chicken holding bowl and toss.

There should be only a smear of oily butter in the pan. Use it to sauté a half small onion, chopped very fine. Keep the onion moving and turn the burner to low. You don't want the onions to brown.

Leaving the onion in the skillet, deglaze the very hot pan with about a cup of half and half cream. Scald the cream and using a wooden spoon, move the onions around. Let the cream rise and fall, lower the heat and reduce about a third.

Into the thickened onion cream, stir a heaping tablespoon of Petite Maison White Truffle Mustard. Again, using your wooden spoon, mix well. Then stir in just a teaspoon of Wildly Delicious Black Maple Magic balsamic vinegar. Combine.

Turn the waiting sautéed chicken pieces and mushrooms, including the collected liquid, into the White Truffle Cream Sauce. Sprinkle with a little more crushed thyme and add finely chopped parsley (dry will work). Use quite a bit, at least a quarter cup. Cover and let the flavors marry. Adjust the seasoning again.

Now add a few slices of fresh peaches. If fresh ones are not available, use tinned peaches (not the ones in unsweetened packing juice). Marinate the tinned peach slices in homemade sugar syrup for a few hours in your *mis en place* preparation. Add lots of pepper. Peaches love pepper. Stir just once to mix. Add to the chicken mix and fold.

Cover and serve over plain buttered basmati rice. Beyond special.

Pair this with my all-time favorite: Sparkling (champagne) rosé, Royal de Neuville, from France. Gourmet never tasted so good. Takes no time to prepare and can be made ahead, but use within a couple of hours. For some reason, this sort of dish changes its chemistry after being refrigerated, and is best served freshly made. But it is still wonderful the second or third day.

In addition: Another way to serve this amazing dish is to change up the presentation by putting a generous portion on an approximate four-inch circle or square of puff pastry, which you have sprinkled with homemade coarse fluffy breadcrumbs as a base. Paint the pastry edges with a little egg wash. Place on a parchment lined cookie sheet, in a 400 F preheated oven just until the pastry puffs. The chicken is already cooked, so it will just warm through.

It's a wonderful, hot *hors d'oeuvres.* You can make smaller puffs or larger ones, or even roll out a pastry dough as you would for a *galette,* and just tuck up and over the pastry edges, leaving the center open; cut into large pie-shaped wedges and serve.

And another way to serve: Prepare wide egg noodles, store-bought or fresh homemade *pappardelle.* (No wide noodles available? Buy store-bought fresh-made pasta lasagna noodles and cut in one-inch-wide portions before cooking.) Or use pasta bowties. Drain well and stir melted butter with fresh chiffonade of basil into the pasta. Another day: Serve with fresh-made (instantly cooked) spaetzle. Mound with the white truffle mustard chicken mix. *So instantly yum!*

And, another easy-do favorite: Serve with a barbecued generous-size portobello mushroom. Prepare the mushroom and transfer it to a hot glass plate. Drizzle the gill side of each mushroom with just a little oil from your marinating goat cheese jar. Mound the gill side of each generous mushroom with the chicken, peach, button mushroom, white truffle mustard mix. Adjust seasonings and serve hot or warm. Remember, a portobello mushroom tastes like steak.

An additional gourmet touch: Sprinkle the stuffed portobello mushroom with fresh, homemade seasoned breadcrumbs: (sage, rosemary and thyme—or just a tiny sprinkle of poultry seasoning in the breadcrumbs), and place under a preheated broiler for just seconds. Another memory maker…enjoy!

For an additional gourmet treat, and for something entirely different: Make a phyllo (filo) pastry ring about four inches or so in diameter, by wrapping the dough around the handle of a wooden spoon; push off the pastry and wrap in a circular position, so it looks a bit like a large donut with a hole. Brush with just a little egg wash. Bake on high heat (400 F) for five minutes or until browned. Brush the pastry with parsley, sage and thyme butter, or melt the herb butter log of your choice from your selection of frozen logs. When the pastry is still hot, fill the center hole in the phyllo pastry, served on a plate, with the chicken mixture, as above.

If you ever make chicken pot pie, substitute this recipe for your regular chicken mix, or enjoy the white truffle mustard sauce chicken (make extra) and then use the leftovers for pot pie. Top with Duchess potatoes, pipe with your forcing bag using a fluted tube, spritz with melted butter and pop under the broiler to flash brown the potatoes. Use a heat-proof French onion soup dish for each pot pie.

Beet Tops and Roasted Red Garden Beets

Beet tops (greens) and roasted red garden beets (or yellow or multi-colored beets). If you love spinach, you will really love this recipe. And the finished dish has multiple uses.

Apparently 99 percent of beet tops (greens) get tossed out. Stores don't even offer them for sale and neither do fresh garden produce shops. The cashier will often say, "Do you want the greens removed, tossed in the trash?" That is such a waste.

Buy fresh beets at the produce market, with the tops on. When you get home, cut off the tops, leaving about two inches of stocks attached. The stocks look a little like rhubarb. Put the beets in the fridge to cook another day.

Wash the greens several times, soaking in cold water. Cut off the red ends of the greens and cook the red stalks separately. Remove center-leaf hard stems from the big floppy green leaves, if they are very rigid.

Start by sautéing the stalks in warm butter and a little salt. You could add a little liquid (water or chicken broth). They take ages to soften. Cover and leave them on the lowest heat to soften; you want them fork tender, mashable. When the stalks are fork tender, add the greens' tops that have been rinsed several times, completely free of all sand.

Add the green tops to the sautéed stems. Cover and let them cook in their own moisture. They take longer to soften and don't wilt easily like spinach does, although they will collapse into the pot and cook down remarkably. A very large bunch of beet greens will reduce to a large cup of finished greens.

When the greens are cooked, drain using a large sieve over a pot. Push the greens to release all the liquid. They won't fully drain on their own. You want them as moisture-free as possible. You might even want to squeeze out any excess moisture using a large fresh white cheesecloth.

Using a cutting board and a sharp large blade chopping knife, crosscut chop, turning the greens and the red cooked stems at angles until the cooked greens resemble cooked, chopped spinach.

In the meantime, chop a small, white onion very fine. Mash a small clove of fresh garlic, mincing it in fresh squeezed lemon juice and salt. Sauté both gently in real butter. Add a tiny sprinkle of salt as you remove it from the sauté pan.

Warm a large tablespoon of butter in the sauté pan. Add a teaspoon of granulated sugar and a tiny pinch of nutmeg. Using a wooden spoon, stir the chopped greens into the warm butter. Add the garlic onion mix.

Now you can save the greens to warm and eat another day, or decide how to eat them immediately. There are many wonderful ways to enjoy them.

At this stage you can even turn the greens into jam or stir them into scalded cream, bagna càuda style, and serve with pasta or use as a crepe filling, or just serve the greens as a delicious, side vegetable dish. Spritz with Marsala wine or a drizzle of Asbach Uralt brandy or any of your favorite bitters spirits. Experiment.

Or, put the greens into a buttered ramekin lined with parchment, and add whisked eggs and cream to make a wonderful treat, baked using a bain-marie. Or you could create Napoleon layering mashed potatoes, cooked ground beef and the greens. Top with a round of frozen butter puff pastry. Serve with a swish of rhubarb confit drizzled over a tablespoon of creamy goat cheese on top while still hot from the oven. (Or top with Wildly Delicious Canadian Red Onion and Beets Marmalade.)

This greens dish is terrific with my whipped mashed potatoes, served with brisket, as you would serve kale—an old Dutch dish (see my kale recipe), alongside tender braised brisket, with its natural juices and a little ordinary white vinegar, or white balsamic (must use).

This beet greens dish is quite a lot of work and might not appeal to all home cooks. This is time-consuming but worth the effort. If you enjoy eating spinach you will likely enjoy beet tops cooked the same way, to start. Then serve in any of several ways. If you haven't eaten beet greens, this recipe is an opportunity to try this special dish that others often throw away. Full of all sorts of good things that your diet might be missing.

In Addition

Make a crostata pastry, savory style. Prepare your favorite pastry. Sprinkle with fresh coarse, homemade breadcrumbs like you use when making strudel, to absorb any moisture. Instead of filling with fruit, fill the open pastry with the cooked beet greens, top with "seared" sliced white, firm, fresh button mushrooms, crisped prosciutto and just a little sweated herbed onion, or dot with cognac marinated baby pearl onions. Pull the sides of the pastry toward the center, leaving the center exposed to the filling, brush the edges with melted butter and bake on high heat (400 F) for 20 minutes. Serve pizza-style wedges, as a terrific veggie-side dish. Maybe great served next to scrambled (barely cooked) eggs, with slices of thawed, frozen, smoked Norwegian salmon on top of the eggs.

Try this delicious dish, using the recipe above:

Individual Roasted Beet Tatin with My Beet Greens recipe

Heat butter in hot skillet. Reduce heat. Add finely chopped shallots. Sauté until fork tender. Stir in a little sugar (maybe a quarter cup) and add a little white balsamic vinegar. Watch chemistry happen. Continue to stir constantly until the sugar congeals.

Layer sliced roasted fresh beets into the caramelized sauce. Rest briefly.

Place a little caramel sauce in the bottom of large, buttered muffin tin. Top with a few layered sauced beet slices. Add some chopped macerated marinated black mission figs from your brandy Asbach Uralt jar. Drizzle just a tiny bit of congealed figgy jus from your marinating jar over top.

Place a generous tablespoon of my beet greens into each muffin tin on top of the beet slices. (I keep a container of cooked beet greens in my freezer. You could freeze them in ice cube trays as individuals; when frozen solid, toss into a plastic bag.)

Top with a frozen puff pastry round, docked to allow to puff beautifully. (Keep the butter puff pastry very cold until ready to bake.) Brush pastry toppers with a little cream, just when putting the pan in the oven.

Bake until the pastry puffs, on high heat, in a preheated oven at 400 F. It won't take long; maybe 8 to 10 minutes.

Tip out the muffin tin. The pastry will be on the bottom. (You could bake in individual buttered ramekins in a water bath.)

Serve on a mound of mixed greens topped with Celebrity label soft, creamy, Canadian goat cheese pucks. (A good opportunity to use your marinated goat cheese pucks.)

Beets love blue cheese, so it's always appropriate to top with blue cheese if you like.

Alternate: Just before topping with butter puff pastry rounds, add a couple of teaspoons of whisked eggs, for a different presentation.

Let's "beet up" the menu…

Chicken Breast Pockets with Red Onion and Beet Marmalade

Marinate large, boneless, skinless chicken breasts for 10 minutes in a little Mazola Corn Oil. Sprinkle with your favorite herbs and spices. I used dried fresh thyme, a little dried fresh mint, a little nutmeg, salt, pepper, and a pinch of garlic salt. Normally I don't use salt when marinating, but this recipe goes fast.

Using a sharp boning knife, slit a pocket into each breast. Fill the pocket with a tablespoon of Red Onion and Beet Marmalade by Wildly Delicious, and put a quarter teaspoon of Dijon in the pocket. A creative use for Petite Maison White Truffle Dijon.

Sauté the chicken breasts in sizzling unsalted butter. First side for four minutes. Set your timer. Turn down the heat and cover at a tilt, or tent with foil and sauté the other side for another three or four minutes, depending on the thickness of the breasts. Check for doneness. Juices need to run clear. But careful not to overcook. Adjust heat. You don't want a crust to form; just a golden surface on the chicken breasts.

While the chicken is sautéing in another skillet, warm the butter until it sizzles, very hot, and add a cup of fresh, tiny, baby, organic white button mushrooms, whole. Sear in the hot butter, just once over easy. You don't want mushy mushrooms. Sprinkle with dried, fresh thyme, a pinch of nutmeg and pepper and don't salt until you are ready to move the mushrooms out of the skillet, to the warm chicken holding platter. Deglaze the skillet with just a little cream and add to the sauce in the chicken skillet just before serving.

Remove the chicken breasts from the skillet immediately when juices run clear and quickly place on a warming platter. Tent to rest. Add about a cup of half and half cream to the hot skillet and let it scald, reducing slightly. Sprinkle with pepper, a little salt, a pinch of nutmeg, just a little fresh lemon juice, a pinch of granulated sugar, a generous tablespoon of bottled, LightHouse brand freeze-dried parsley (or fresh if you have it) and a quarter teaspoon of White Truffle Dijon, stirring constantly. Turn off the heat. Now add a couple of generous tablespoons of the Red Onion and Beet Marmalade to the sauce. Stir gently. Turn down the heat but keep the sauce warm. It will continue to thicken. (You could substitute your own homemade kumquat marmalade that you made using my recipe.)

Make a generous puddle of the serving sauce on a large, white or black plate (yes, the chicken is golden white), but you want to show off your beet sauce. Not only is this sauce amazing, it is good for you. Gently position the chicken breasts on the puddle. Keep the plates warm in a low heat preheated oven if necessary.

Serve with a side plate of whipped mashed potatoes and sliced roasted fresh from the garden beets, spritzed with Black Maple Magic Balsamic Vinegar. You can add a tablespoon of the beet greens to the pocket you made in the chicken breasts, before sauté.

Alternate serving idea: Meanwhile, toast six baguette slices (or more), or three full-size slices of black-olive bread for each person. Butter the toasts. Smear with homemade oven-roasted garlic puree. Place on hot, individual serving oval or rectangular platters and position thick slices of chicken breasts on top of the toasts. Pour the thick special sauce and the whole mushrooms over top. The bread will soak up some of the sauce.

For a king-size special "beet" celebration meal, you could add my Boston Bibb lettuce salad, with warm, blue cheese dressing, served with Kuhne brand whole baby beets.

Decadent Pancakes Gourmet Topper: Apples or Green Tomatoes [close up] or Bing Cherries

You can make this topping ahead of time and heat to serve. You want to serve this topping almost hot.

Core and sauté coarsely chopped firm apples, in very hot butter. I love firm Delicious apples and a more or less matching amount of chopped Spanish onion. About equal portions.

Fry full fat slices of bacon, chopped coarsely in about one-inch pieces, until almost but not quite crispy. Add a little fresh rosemary and a pinch of fresh thyme. The flavors will explode in the mouth. Put everything back into the skillet.

Flambé the apple mix with your favorite cognac. If you have a marinated black mission fig jar, stir in a mashed, minced marinated fig and a tablespoon of the jar cognac liquid.

Sprinkle with just a little salt. Apples like salt; it brings out their flavor.

Pour a little double reduced maple syrup crème anglaise over the mixture as you mound the apple mix over freshly made dinner-plate size pancakes. Don't make the pancakes too thick. Add a tiny bit of the hot bacon fat, drizzled over top, and grate a bit of orange peel on top. Or chop a few pieces of your candied orange peel strips you keep on hand in a sugar jar.

Don't overcook the pancakes. Try buckwheat or buttermilk pancakes, freshly made. Keep them warm in a large chafing dish or in the oven.

This topping is also great on French toast, and/or as a crepe filling. And don't forget to try it on homemade waffles.

A nice drink with this dish is freshly made hot chocolate topped with a big spoon of Grand Marnier flavored Chantilly cream.

Now for a more savory topping: Simply replace the apples with firm, green tomatoes, seeded and chopped. Sautéed just briefly, once over lightly. You don't want them to turn to mush. Use the reduced maple anglaise sauce, but add a few generous grinds of fresh ground cracked black pepper, and just follow the rest of the recipe. Amazing use for fresh green tomatoes. First ones on the vine as soon as they are ripe.

Now, if you really, really want decadence, try this. Replace the apples with Bing cherries (absolutely not cherry pie filling).

I always have bottled Bing cherries in my pantry. These are dark burgundy or mahogany colored cherries. The kind used for authentic Black Forest cake. Of course, you can use fresh Bing cherries in season, or if available in your area. Using fresh cherries, cook them in light sugar syrup until they just wilt a bit.

I thicken the bottled cherries and juice using a little cornstarch because I don't want to reduce the juice. Stir in real, authentic *kirschwasser*. There are no substitutes for it. Add to the sautéed onions. The fresh rosemary goes nicely with the cherries for a sweet rustic flavor. Flavor the crème anglaise with Marsala.

Note: Another time, over the cherries, pour sabayon or zabaglione, flavored with Marsala. Turn this breakfast or brunch—pancakes, crepes, or waffles—into a dinner meal, as an accompaniment to my Marsala chicken. This wonderful Bing cherry recipe goes perfectly with roast venison or with roasted lamb chops, too. For those who enjoy duck, give it a try, too.

Here's a link to my Marsala chicken REM recipe.

http://www.remonline.com/gourmet-recipes-real-estate-professionals-marsala-chicken/

The first time I published this, a colleague sent me a "delicious note," saying she had replicated my recipe in her own real estate newsletter. Readers are welcome to do so, but because my recipes are part of my manuscript, kindly honor the copyright.

Simply *YUM* gourmet.

Canada's Fiddleheads ~ A Sure Sign of spring

Add to your recipe repertoire: A most unusual treat indeed. As Canadian as the Canada goose, the loon, the beaver, Canadian bacon, Canadian maple syrup and the Bloody Caesar.

During birthday 150 for Canada, make any of these delightful fiddlehead offerings…but remember, it's a totally seasonal thing; fiddleheads are only available, picked fresh, in Canada's east coast in the spring.

(Scroll down, for Lady Ralston's personal Cream of Fiddlehead Soup recipe.)

Just one idea of many: Use my vichyssoise recipe (see below) and float on each wide, flat, deep soup plate, the properly cooked, coiled fiddleheads. They must be carefully cleaned, gently poached twice in fresh, salted water (toss away the poaching liquid) for about seven minutes or less each time, then bathed in ice water to stop the cooking and keep the delightful natural green fern color of the fiddleheads. Then sauté and drizzle in hot unsalted butter; melt a butter puck from your frozen herb butter log always on hand, and drizzle over the hot sautéed, fresh picked, never frozen, fiddleheads.

If you are not going to float your fiddleheads in my vichyssoise, or use them instead of leeks, making my most delicate Cream of Fiddlehead Soup, perhaps invite your guests to share the fiddleheads as a side dish, drizzled with just a little of my warm, blue cheese salad dressing. Or alongside a grilled Portobello mushroom (the Portobello tastes like steak, truly.) Maybe even stuff the Portobello with cooked, fresh, crab meat and homemade coarse, seasoned breadcrumbs, served alongside the fiddleheads side dish. This won't work well with store-bought breadcrumbs.

Fiddleheads, the tiny curled frond of the fern family, taste a little like earthy asparagus, and can sometimes replicate the moisture fragrance of soggy peat marsh soil. Fiddleheads can be poisonous if not cooked properly. But for people from New Brunswick to Maine and parts of Quebec, gourmands wait anxiously for the short-lived spring feasts of this native green (fern) vegetable.

If you would like an accompaniment, may I suggest a ramekin (prepared ahead of time, covered, and refrigerated overnight is okay, then served at room temperature) filled serving cup of my garlic, fresh, shelled (after sauté), medium-size shrimp, sautéed in real garlic, slivered, and mashed with butter. (You can deglaze the sauté pan with your choosing, but Asbach Uralt brandy performs well.) Add the just barely cooked shrimp (peel the shells after the shrimp are sautéed, before you add the shrimp to the cream sauce), bathed in my garlic cream bagna càuda sauce. Include a portion of toasted black-olive baguette, smeared with unsweetened butter or an herb butter puck. As a gourmand addition, it makes for a sometimes earth-moving eating experience like no other.

Vichyssoise (1972) Leek Soup, Pureed ~ with real cream (or make it as Lady Ralston's personal Cream of Fiddlehead Soup)

To make this soup into a fiddlehead cream soup, simply replace the leek with fiddleheads, washed and simmered (twice) and sautéed in hot unsalted butter. Add the pre-sautéed fiddleheads separately to the sautéed onions and proceed as with the vichyssoise recipe.

Sauté rinsed (get rid of ALL the sand completely and carefully) chopped leaks. I use three, tall, generous-sizes leek stalks, or four skinny ones. Use all but the very top, dark, inedible, bruised, dark green rubbery pieces—other people use only the white part. I try hard not to waste anything that is at all edible, and I don't mind the additional flavor imparted by the mid-green section. I cut each stalk into three or four pieces, then split lengthwise to get the sand out. Often, leeks are full of fine sand even when you don't see it. Change the rinsing water a few times and each time, you will see the sand residue.

Add to the sauté pot, a small, white onion, (about a half-cup size) cut in quarters and a clove of garlic (small, skin removed, not crushed). Leave it whole, it will disappear. Add a sprinkle of dry thyme, a pinch of salt and a sprinkle of fine pepper. Not much of either. You can add more later.

Don't let the pot burn. Use medium-high heat to sear the leeks and onions, but not completely brown them. Watch closely. Stir if the leeks and onions stick to the pot. When the leek and the onions are almost soft, add a couple of cups of homemade chicken stock (never from a box, those products no matter what brand are too briny) and three small potatoes; quartered. Don't try to extend the volume by adding extra potatoes; that will make the soup gummy.

That's it. When the potatoes are almost soft, not mushy, turn off the heat and purée in a food processor or blender. At this point, you can leave the base in the fridge overnight or even freeze the base. It will keep for ages to provide an instant gourmet soup on a busy day when you don't feel like cooking. Readymade "gourmet."

In a new pot, on high heat, scald half and half cream. Be careful not to burn the cream. Lift the pan off the heat from time to time. The amount of cream depends on how much of the base you are going to use. For the whole pot, I would not use more than a cup and a half of half and half cream. Or a 1:3 mix of cream to base.

Let the cream come to a soft boil in a large pot. Watch it *very* closely. Don't leave the stove. It will puff up and want to overspill the sides of the pot. Just lift the pot off the heat. Let the cream puff up about three or four times. It will automatically thicken as it fills the pot and recedes.

Remove the cream pot from the burner. Then using a large ladle, scoop the leek mixture into the hot cream and stir gently until heated through. Do not boil. The cream will separate and make a mess. Just warm through. Adjust the seasoning if necessary. You cannot freeze the soup with the cream in. I tried it—the mixture goes watery. If you have frozen the base, mash it with a potato masher to bring to a consistency where you can add it to scalded hot cream. Then whisk gently or stir with a wooden spoon. Heat. Do not boil.

It always tastes better the next day. It will keep in the fridge for a few days and can be reheated very gently, even over a pot of hot (not boiling) water in a bain-marie. The cream soup will stick and burn easily in the pot if you aren't very careful using direct burner heat.

2017 update: "Up-Gourmet" my spectacular vichyssoise soup by adding a drizzle of your Asbach Uralt cognac marinating jus from your black mission fig jar, just when ready to serve. Decorate each serving with a medium-large fresh, green, fried basil leaf, propped in the center of the soup plate, or a large, fresh, fried, mint leaf. Or split a marinated black mission fig from your jar and center it in the soup bowl. *Very yum!*

I don't much care for what Julia Child insisted in the making of her soups. I don't follow her recipes. Some people say that her method of using roux and velouté to thicken cream soups works for them. It's much better, in my opinion, to use real cream and no flour.

How About: Maybe A Fiddlehead Salad

Perhaps make your favorite hollandaise sauce, made with wilted finely chopped shallots, beurre blanc, drizzled over sautéed fiddleheads in unsalted butter, with a squeeze of fresh lemon and a bit of lemon zest.

Fan a sliced, pitted fresh plump avocado, spritzed with lemon and lots of fresh grated pepper and a little salt; drizzle with your favorite, white, balsamic vinegar. And add a few brightly colored edible flowers (maybe violets and nasturtiums for a nice color mix) to a pretty see-through glass plate.

Twist a few paper-thin prosciutto slices into loose rose-like shapes around the edges of the plates. As an alternate or in addition, peel a fresh, juicy cantaloupe, or a papaya, and slice in generous slices and add to each salad plate.

If serving on a buffet table, print the word *Fiddleheads* in cursive, on a tiny label and wrap the label on a stable toothpick inserted into each salad plate.

And then there is the *pièce de résistance*: Prepare your favorite beer batter and deep fry fiddlehead coils that you have poached and sautéed first. Salt immediately. Eat right away. Or as an alternative, try dredging cooked, individual fiddleheads in seasoned all-purpose flour or even semolina, egg wash and coarse, fresh, homemade breadcrumbs, and deep fry. Salt while hot. Mouthwatering treat, for sure.

Dine in Tails: Lobster Tails That Is…

Lobster tails in white truffle mustard homemade mayo sauce.

This is a perfect Sunday brunch. Or celebrate a special birthday, perhaps. Two five-inch tails make about a cup of chopped lobster pieces.

This is a perfect Sunday brunch. Or celebrate a special birthday, perhaps. Two five-inch tails make about a cup of chopped lobster pieces.

Poach fresh or thawed frozen lobster tails in a large covered pot of gently boiling salted water. Depending on the tail size, four minutes should be about right. Often recipes call for 10 to 12 minutes. I always found that that was too long to cook. Don't want rubber lobster. Remember the seafood will keep on cooking in its own heat when you remove it from the hot water. Let the water come to a roaring boil, slip the tails in, cover at a tilt and turn down the heat to create a soft rolling boil. Set your timer. Don't walk away from the stove.

Using tongs, remove the tails to a plate. Using lobster shears or sharp kitchen shears, split the top shell in half, lengthwise. Pull apart the shell and remove the meat. Cut the lobster in bite-size pieces. Let it cool completely. Drizzle the lobster meat with a just a little of the leftover oil from your goat cheese marinating jar. Don't have any leftover fresh oils? Use your favorite oil. A little Maplewood Grape seed sunflower mix from Wildly Delicious works. Warm, melted unsalted butter will do nicely.

In homemade mayonnaise, stir in a little Petite Maison White Truffle Mustard. Add a little pinch of plain white sugar, lots of fresh, cracked, black pepper and a pinch of salt.

Sprinkle just a little sweet paprika and a tiny pinch of fresh dried thyme. Mince fine a little chiffonade of fresh parsley and a tiny bit of fresh tarragon, if you enjoy the fresh herbs. It's fine even without. You could add a little finely chopped crispy fresh celery and just a tiny bit of the celery leaves. Be careful with celery—it can overtake other flavors easily.

Pour the mayo mix over the chopped cooled lobster. Refrigerate, covered tightly in a glass container, overnight to give time for the flavors to marry. Stir gently, just once. Serve on a small fresh, buttered, warm, soft, Parker House dinner roll.

Plate with a fanned half fresh avocado, spritzed with fresh squeezed lemon, a little salt and fresh ground pepper. Drizzle with a little Wildly Delicious Maplewood grape seed oil, or your favorite oil and a little white balsamic vinegar.

A perfect pairing with my all-time favorite crackling French sparkling rose, Royal de Neuville. Just the right balance as a palate cleanser between bites.

Alternate: Put a little butter in a hot skillet. Toss poached lobster pieces for just seconds. Flambé the hot lobster with Asbach Uralt cognac. Let cool and add to the mayo mix. Refrigerate overnight and drizzle with a little cognac marinating jus from your black mission fig Asbach Uralt marinating jar, just when ready to serve. You could even add a little finely chopped macerated fig pieces.

Not up for poaching lobster? (It's easier than you might think.) There are a few brands of great tinned frozen lobster. Some are better than others. It's sometimes difficult to find best one, packed in St. Anne, Que. A large tin (a generous cup) is often about $25 to $30. Or, buy a cooked fresh lobster with large claws. Use only the claw meat for this salad. Experiment. Enjoy this really delightful brunch. Your friends will want a recipe copy. Simple, easy, tasty gourmet. It has a most unusual taste and perhaps for some is an "acquired" taste, not unlike olives or anchovies. Gentle warning: It could be addictive.

Bell Peppers Lobster

Another great *hors d'oeuvre*: Roast multi-colored, very large bell peppers on your grill or stove top if you have a gas range. Split the peppers and remove the seeds. I leave the roasted skins on. A wonderful flavor that cannot be mistaken. Remember when cutting, slice bell peppers skin side up, or you could cause the peppers to be bitter. Slice the large roasted peppers vertically, using a sharp, serrated knife, into quite wide strips.

Position a little lobster salad on the end of each strip. Have party picks ready. Roll the soft but not mushy pepper strips around and around the lobster bit. Stick with the toothpick to keep closed. Position the pinwheels open side up and bake in a hot oven for only 10 minutes to just prepare a warm *hors d'oeuvre*. Or, do the tri-part routine and dredge the pepper pinwheels in seasoned flour, egg wash and fresh coarse breadcrumbs (try making them from black-olive bread dried leftovers; save and freeze the bread until you have enough to make crumbs). By the way, off topic: Stir a little of the black olive breadcrumbs into partially mashed cooked Brussels sprouts for a divine experience.

Deep fry the bell pepper pinwheel rolls in hot (350 F) Mazola Corn Oil just until the crumbs are golden. Salt immediately while still hot. Serve on a large platter alongside crispy raw Belgian endive with a little lobster mix on the blunt end. A total lobster treat.

The list is just endless for making various uses of your terrific lobster mix. Before mixing with your homemade mayo, pull the lobster meat into small pieces and flambé with Asbach Uralt. Then mix the flambéed lobster pieces, cooled, into my Canadian Cheese ball, or my Asbach Cheese ball, along with the existing recipe for a true birthday Canada Day celebration.

Lobster Lunch and Blini

And here's a birthday treat I made for a friend's special day: Lobster lunch and blini.

It's a gourmet treat. It's a sweet lobster lunch (small tails frozen, thawed and steamed over chicken broth). Add couple of whole garlic cloves to the chicken broth. Mash them in the sauce later if you like. Remove the lobster meat from shells.

Melt butter in a skillet and add warm lobster pieces. Flambé in very good European brandy/cognac—I use Asbach Uralt, but it has been delisted. I stocked up ages ago; no idea what to replace it with. Remove the lobster.

Reduce juices just a little; add cream and scald to thicken. Stir in soft poached garlic; mashed. Reintroduce the lobster and cracked black pepper. The meat is almost sweet. Serve warm, in your best crystal shrimp cocktail glass. Really yum.

This amazing lobster salad recipe is also a great filler for crepes. Just make sure the sauce is thickened. You can use as much or as little lobster meat as you like. You can even buy precooked lobster and just gently reheat in butter and flambé. Drizzle with brandy figgy jus, and mash a couple of macerated, marinated in Asbach Uralt brandy, black mission figs.

Another time, I might add gelatin to the lobster salad and let it set up in individual small molds. Serve on a large hydroponically grown Boston Bibb lettuce leaf.

You can also pulse the cooked lobster, add a tiny bit of cream, a sprig of thyme and fresh basil. Rough chop in the blender and make blini. Serve with a tiny dollop of sour cream and a tarragon or fresh basil plant leaf to decorate the plate. Overlap three blini, about three-inch diameter, in your plate presentation.

Pair with a light dessert such as freshly made sabayon or even plain panna cotta, drizzled with a little brandy figgy jus. Top it with a split in half Asbach Uralt brandy marinated whole firm fresh, not dried, black mission fig, served in a wide mouth stem champagne crystal glass.

For an additional gourmet treat and for something entirely different: Make a phyllo (filo) pastry ring about four inches or so in diameter, by wrapping the dough around the handle of a wooden spoon. Push off the pastry and wrap in a circular position, so it looks a bit like a large donut with a hole. Brush with just a little egg wash. Bake on high heat (400 F) for five minutes or until browned. Brush the pastry with tarragon butter or the herb butter log of your choice from your selection on hand of frozen herbed butter logs. When cooled to room temperature, fill the center hole in the Phyllo pastry, served on a plate, with the lobster tails mixture as above.

Ready-Cooked Frozen Shrimp in Ghee Crème

Since shrimp typically is not an inexpensive item, why not make sure you prepare it properly? Cooked properly you will enjoy every bite.

Often people overcook shrimp or are afraid to try to cook it. Overcooked anything is usually awful. Shrimp and scallops can bounce like rubber balls when overcooked in a sauté, or get terribly chewy on a barbecue or when done on a grill. Since shrimp typically is not an inexpensive item, why not make sure you prepare it properly? Cooked properly, you will enjoy every bite.

Just don't overcook it. Remember that as with most foods, cooking continues after removing it from the heat source.

How do you not overcook shrimp that is already cooked? For starters forget about the microwave.

Let's start with ghee. Called by any other name it's really just clarified butter. Most people make their ghee using salt butter, but when you only have unsalted butter, just prepare your ghee the same way. It's ready in minutes and can be used right away and/or kept for several days, even unrefrigerated. Makes a great camping or travel cooking companion.

The idea is to warm the butter through. You aren't cooking the butter. And simply remove the milk solids. Some people strain it through clean, never before used cheesecloth, but I prefer to just pour off the liquid or scoop it out with a large metal serving spoon, leaving the milk solids behind. Ideally use a stainless-steel pan. The ghee will keep for ages unrefrigerated and cooking with it, since it has a higher smoke point than regular butter, is truly a gift.

Don't throw away the milk solids. They are good for topping veggies or pasta dishes or to add to cream sauces, among other uses.

Note: A skillet with higher sides will allow steam to help cook or warm its contents and sometimes you want that; a skillet with low sides lets the steam escape and creates a different cooking environment.

Choose your pots and pans carefully. Each kitchen should have more than one of each, and several sizes—each has a use. You can cook remarkable dishes using any old tin pan. But if you want ideal results, choose specifics. They are designed with a purpose in mind. As you progress in your cooking skills, over time, you will learn to notice the difference such small attention makes.

To Prepare the Frozen Shrimp

Start by putting enough ghee in a hot skillet with higher sides, to just barely coat the pan. You just want a slippery surface, in this case. Not a ghee flood. The smoke point is very high, like good oil. Ghee does not burn easily, but it will if you don't watch. Throw it out and start again if you find the ghee has burned or turned dark brown. Simply carefully wipe out the skillet completely using a paper towel and start again.

When the ghee is very hot, lift the skillet from the heat source and add the already cooked, barely thawed, still cold frozen shrimp. Tails on is fine.

Shake the skillet a little so all the pre-cooked frozen, thawed shrimp, in one layer, get a little ghee on. You have turned off the heat but now put the hot pan back on the still-hot burner.

Watch the shrimp carefully for just a few minutes. You just want to heat it through. Remember the shrimp is already cooked. As it is heating, sprinkle generously with garlic salt and ground sweet paprika. Use high quality pepper and add plenty. Shake the pan to coat the warmed shrimp. No need to add salt. The shrimp is already plenty salty.

Remove the shrimp from the skillet, using a slotted spoon. Deglaze with your favorite spirits: a generous half cup. Pernod, or dry white wine, or cognac. Or an extra special treat: deglaze with Chartreuse monk bitters. Let the alcohol burn off until nearly completely vaporized. I use a piece of folded paper towel at this point, to stick any bits of shell and keep the sauce completely shell-free. A few bits of the tail shells sometimes disengage from the shrimp while warming in the hot ghee.

Note: Add a cup of half and half cream to the very hot skillet. Bring to a slow gentle boil. Scald the cream and let reduce slightly. Stir into the thickened cream a half teaspoon of Dijon mustard. Stir in two tablespoons of Applewood Hickory Smoke barbecue sauce.

If you have made my spectacular leftover tomato barbecue sauce, this is an ideal use for it (http://www.remonline.com/recipes-busy-sales-reps-spectacular-barbecue-serving-sauce/)

You might want to add a little sambal tomato sauce to my tomato barbecue sauce because it is a little milder than with the Applewood sauce. You could also use my tomato butter if you have some on hand; the sauce will be different, a little sweet, but still wonderful.

Return the warmed shrimp to the sauce. Stir to coat. Using a rubber spatula so you don't waste a drop, put the shrimp and the sauce into a glass warming dish. Serve immediately or refrigerate to serve cold later.

Decide how you will serve it. Do not reheat in the sauce. If cold, then just serve cold, or even at room temperature. Each method of serving is different but equally delicious. This is a simple, amazing dish that you will make regularly.

Either way, when ready to eat, sprinkle a chiffonade of fresh basil over top.

The cream sauce leaves a nice sated oil covering in your mouth. The mix of the garlic salt, paprika, plenty of great fragrant pepper, Dijon and the smoky barbecue sauce creates the most amazing combination.

Of course, you could sauté uncooked, fresh, never frozen shrimp in ghee and proceed with the ghee sauce as well. As with my other recipe for shrimp cooked in their shells, you can "pot" this ghee shrimp as well. The ghee cream will firm up but remain soft and is delectable as an everyday treat. If you have leftover sauce, use it on your favorite gnocchi or pasta. And serve with any kind of seafood.

A frosted glass of cool Winzertanz pairs well with this, as does my old standby, French pink champagne-like, crackling rose Royal de Neuville.

Preparation takes no time at all and there are dozens of ways to serve. Or just eat it all, by yourself, as finger food, with a large napkin to catch the drips, as a TV movie night treat. Mop up sauce with toasted crustless ordinary bread triangle pieces.

It's wonderful with plain instant one-minute basmati rice or with zucchini slivered to look like spaghetti. Try the warmed pre-cooked, frozen shrimp as a mix with large al dente pasta seashells. It's a really special treat no matter which way you choose to eat it. Incredibly delicious. So very melt in your mouth rich.

Alternate: If you really want to get creative, pull the tails off the sauced shrimp. Toss the whole thing into your kitchen machine and pulse. Add whole eggs and a little cream until you get a thick pourable paste, sort of like a very thick pancake batter. Butter ramekins and place a cooked lobster claw or a piece of cooked crab claw meat, or even a sautéed sea scallop, in each.

Fill with the shrimp cream paste, just three-quarters full. Place the ramekins in a bain-marie pan in a medium heat oven until the sauce congeals. Empty each ramekin upside down on a pretty plate and drizzle with a little ghee, or serve in a tiny ghee puddle. Decorate each plate with a sprig of fresh basil leaves and a lemon curl. Add a vine of crunchy frozen, green sweet seedless grapes and enjoy.

You can also make ghee cream shrimp quenelles and poach very carefully. Remember, everything is already cooked. You are just heating it through. A perfect seafood accompaniment alongside seared large sea scallops, with homemade gnocchi.

Chicken Escalope Au Figue

...And simply a figgy gem gourmet dessert experience, too.

Fig or fique. In any language it spells "wonderful." Figs are now readily available in most supermarkets—there was a time when we couldn't get them. They don't have a long shelf life, so some supermarkets are reluctant to carry them.

If you want to feed four a generous helping of chicken, this recipe is simple to make. It cooks quickly and disappears from the dinner plate even quicker.

Start by having two fresh, never frozen, generous, boneless, skinless, chicken breasts, each cut into three equal portions. Pound the chicken pieces out a little but not as much as if you were preparing schnitzel. Just to enlarge the pieces for equalizing cooking time.

Sprinkle the chicken with just a tiny bit of Mazola Corn Oil, salt, pepper and a little garlic salt. Add just a pinch of nutmeg and a little crushed dried thyme. (It's just my personal preference, but I don't like olive oil on chicken; I taste the olives. I love olives but not the flavor imparted into my chicken.)

To hot butter in the skillet, add a little piece of "poached in chicken stock" garlic cloves from your garlic that's stored in an oil bottle. Don't mash the garlic yet. Just leave the clove whole. Be careful not to brown the garlic.

Heat a wide skillet that has low sides and add a little clarified butter and a little Mazola Corn Oil. Not much oil. Just enough to coat the skillet. Be careful not to brown. Lower heat just a little, to medium. Lift the skillet from the burner briefly. Place each piece of chicken in the skillet so they are not touching one another.

When the underside of each piece of chicken turns a light golden color, it's time to turn each piece, one by one. Don't leave the stove. Keep your eye on the chicken. It cooks very quickly. It's fork-tender. Flambé with a half cup of Asbach Uralt cognac. That's a sizeable amount of brandy. Stand back so you don't get singed.

Note: Never pour spirits into a hot skillet directly from the liquor bottle. Never! Instead use a cup with a pouring lip so the cup doesn't drip dangerously. The alcohol will light itself naturally from the heat of the skillet.

Many homeowners are fortunate to have a cooking island that houses their cooktop burners, with nothing overhead. Other kitchens have cabinets and/or a built-in microwave quite close to the cooking surface of the stove. If that is your kitchen, perhaps when lighting a flambé, set the very hot pan off the stovetop immediately before lighting, briefly until the alcohol burns off. If you practice being careful, there's no need to be afraid to flambé.

Cooking Attire

If you have loose, long hair, tie it up or back when working with food, especially so when working with an open flame. And nothing is more unappetizing than finding a hair in food. It's an interesting situation on tv cooking shows where often long hair (both men and women) is falling forward and is practically in the food. I'm surprised the producers don't address that. Falling hair bits can't be helped, but surely no one wants to find strands of hair in food. The only way to avoid it is to do as above, or wear a hairnet when preparing food. Never put a tea towel over your shoulder. Bits of dandruff or hair live there on your shoulders.

Likewise, be careful when working with floppy, long sleeves or wearing a Sunday morning dressing gown. They are fire hazards. And splatters can ruin clothing.

Ages ago, I found a wonderful loose-fitting lab coat with three-quarter length sleeves and snap closures, made of manmade, flame-resistant fabric that is really wash and wear. Splatters don't adhere to it, and if I find the need to cook while wearing good clothes, I can cover up entirely. A most valuable kitchen investment, much better than an apron. And you don't want your cover-up to have floppy long sleeves, either, but you do want your arms covered against splatters that can burn.

Speaking of safety, keep animals out of the kitchen when you are cooking, particularly when preparing flambé. It's no time for Fido to park at your feet. Likewise, caution prevails when you are deep-frying.

Absolutely do not overcook the chicken escalope. Remove the chicken pieces to a warming platter immediately when test juices run clear. Let the brandy reduce. Add a half cup of figgy jus from your cognac black mission fig marinating jar and scrape any stuck-on bits.

Add a cup of cream and scald, letting the cream thicken just a little. Adjust seasonings.

Coarsely chop a cup of marinated but not macerated black mission figs from your Asbach Uralt cognac marinating jar. Add to the cream sauce and pour over the warm chicken platter.

For dessert, serve my figgy panna cotta or figgy zabaglione. And enjoy with a cup of fresh brewed coffee or espresso.

Alternate: Replace the Asbach Uralt with Italian red Marsala wine for a whole different dish. Marsala wine lives in a world all its own, like no other.

Serve the chicken, covered in sauce, with homemade gnocchi or with homemade spaetzle. You can have prepped the homemade gnocchi earlier, and even have it frozen, ready to slide into a pot of boiling salted water. It's ready in minutes without thawing. The spaetzle needs to be made and eaten right away, ideally. Drain in a colander, or remove with a slotted spoon or spider. Drizzle with hot, melted butter or top with pucks of one of your frozen herb butters, or even top with your marinated Celebrity goat cheese pucks; the heat of the pasta will melt the cheese. If serving with gnocchi, offer the chicken *escalopes* on the side of a wide, low soup plate.

If, per chance, you have leftover gnocchi in sauce, reheat it gently for lunch the next day, using a bain-marie. A crispy toasted, buttered slice of black-olive bread alongside completes a tasty leftovers lunch.

For a special side dish flavor-pairing, or dessert, serve baked stuffed figs. Using a sharp paring knife, hollow out the bottom of each fig, making just a little round hole. Mash a log of plain, Celebrity label, Canadian goat cheese and stir in fresh, crushed, candied walnuts from your pantry jar. Mince a little candied citrus rind from your citrus sugar pantry jar and stir into the nutty goat cheese. Using a decorating forcing bag, with a hole that matches the size of the whole fresh fig hole you've created, force the cheese mixture into the bottom of each fig.

Make sure the generous fresh figs are positioned in a baking dish, so that the figs stand up and are not able to fall over. Pop into a 400 F oven for about eight minutes. Watch closely. After you remove the hot figs, drizzle them with figgy jus from your cognac marinating jar. And don't waste any drippings in the baking dish.

Use a large soup serving spoon to remove each fig. Position each stuffed fig in a bowl of Chantilly Cream, or onto a small bed of soft, warm baked brie cheese. Topping with a scoop of homemade vanilla ice cream would work.

Perhaps serve in a wide-mouth old-fashioned champagne stem glass, the kind of glass no one uses for champagne anymore. Served with my all-time favorite, sparking pink (champagne) in a stem flute, French Royal de Neuville, this gem could easily become a habit.

Battered Deep-Fried Halibut Steak Nuggets

It's a fishy thing…(Consider the onions)

Get your butcher to cut a two-inch or three-inch-thick steak, cut from just below the gills of a full-size fresh halibut. It's called a center cut steak.

You might have to pay him extra, and halibut is already expensive, but tell him you need one or two-inch "nuggets" cut from that steak. Ask him to remove the skin first. When you get the fresh, never frozen fish nuggets home, check for any missed bones. Remove with tweezers or needle-nose pliers. Check carefully using your fingers.

When ready to cook, sprinkle the nuggets with ground pepper, crushed thyme, just a pinch of garlic powder, a little minced fresh dill and a bit of paprika. No salt. You can salt when the fish is cooked.

I only deep fry in Mazola Corn Oil. I am aware of the situation with corn genetic engineering, but it is still the best oil for this purpose. Mazola is cholesterol free.

Never fill your pot more than half full of oil. Never! And never cover to speed up the heating process. Do not ever leave the stove when deep-frying, not even for a minute.

There should be no reason to fear deep-frying, but common sense needs to be in place constantly. Get everything you need organized ahead of time. You don't want to go looking for the slotted spoon when it's time to use it. *Mis en place.*

In another recipe, I noted that I keep an old, real wool, thick blanket tucked away in my kitchen within easy reach of the stove. If you ever experience a stovetop kitchen fire, place the wool blanket over the stovetop. The wool helps smother the flames and is slow to burn, but the blanket must be real wool, not synthetic. A fire extinguisher in the kitchen is ideal, but you must be able to lift it and know how to use it. If you need it, that's no time to start reading instructions.

Reserve a special pot only for deep-frying, even if you don't use it often. Heat your deep fry oil in a heavy, enamel-coated, cast-iron pot if you don't have a deep fryer, while you prepare your batter. Test the oil for 350 F or by dropping in a cube of bread.

Prepare your favorite batter. I like to use my Chinese shrimp batter, so easy to make and always has a consistent result. It's a little like a tempura batter. The batter looks a little like thick pancake prep but it poofs in the hot oil and gets to a beautiful golden color quickly and the very light finished texture is wonderful. Most things are cooked when the batter turns golden. Refer to my deep-fried vegetables and even deep-fried ice cream.

Carefully deep fry a few nuggets at a time, turning with a slotted spoon. Remove the nuggets from the hot oil as soon as the batter gets to a beautiful golden color on all sides. Keep turning them so the nuggets cook consistently.

The halibut is very fragile and cooks quickly. Remember, the fish will continue cooking in its own heat while resting. Absolutely do not overcook.

Drain on a paper towel. (Never use the brown paper towel sheets in your kitchen.) Sprinkle the deep-fried halibut nuggets with lots of salt. If you like, sprinkle with sweet paprika and/or cayenne.

Squeeze fresh lemon juice over the nuggets just before serving, or add a tiny pot of fresh lemon zest to each serving plate, along with lemon wedges so people can serve themselves.

If you enjoy a dipper sauce, use your favorite. For me, a dab of Dijon works nicely. Even on the second day for leftovers.

The halibut nuggets will melt in your mouth. A true gourmet delight.

Serve with fresh, thick, sliced tomatoes and crispy iceberg lettuce drizzled with my warm blue cheese dressing.

Alternate: Another time, marinate the halibut steak and leave it in one piece. Marinate for 20 minutes before grilling or pan frying.

For fresh wonderful marinade, whisk a third cup of your favorite oil with a third cup of fresh squeezed lemon juice, a quarter cup of finely chopped fresh parsley, a pinch of dried thyme, a tiny bit of mustard and fresh ground pepper. No salt. Stir in a teaspoon of very finely chopped onion or green onion.

Pour it over the halibut steak. Turn once only in the marinade.

When ready to grill or pan fry, dab the steak with paper towel to soak up a little of the marinade and dry off the steak.

Pan fry quickly on medium high heat in butter only. There's enough oil on the fish from the marinade. You can also grill the whole halibut steak. It cooks very quickly. Or you can barbecue the halibut steak in a papillote.

Serve with a beautiful choice of fresh thinly sliced cucumber that you have salted and rinsed, and fresh, chopped, dill in sour cream, or thinly sliced peppery radishes marinated briefly in salt, pepper and white balsamic vinegar. No oil.

Another Alternate: Dredge the halibut steak in seasoned flour. Tap off excess flour. Dip the whole steak in egg wash. Then lay the large steak in a tray of homemade breadcrumbs. Cover completely. (This doesn't work well with store-bought crumbs.)

You will want to move quickly. Pan fry in butter and oil mix, or barbecue using a special grill sheet.

You might find a tall glass of your favorite beer or a cool glass of white wine is a good pairing.

Roast that Large Mouth Bass

If it's bass fishing season, you might like to check out my 1970s newspaper column *Gourmet Cooking with Carolyne* recipe for large-mouth bass:

After you have cleaned your catch, store it at home in the coldest part of the fridge, in double tinfoil that is not completely sealed, until you are ready to cook. Let it air-breathe.

Preheat the oven to 350 F. Rinse three to four pounds of fish under very cold running water and sprinkle with lots of lemon juice, inside and out.

Salt with freshly ground sea salt and freshly ground pepper. Place a tablespoon of herb butter inside the belly and two more tablespoons in the roasting pan. Place the fish on its side in the pan, where you have completely covered the bottom of the pan with sliced raw lemons and onion slices.

Pop into the oven and baste every 10 minutes with the melted butter in the bottom of the pan.

Allow about a half hour to 40 minutes roasting time. Just 10 minutes before removing it from the oven, add a cup of Winzertanz.

The whole fish is cooked when it flakes. Rest, tented, before serving.

Arrange the whole bass on a bed of fresh parsley and garnish with lemon wedges. Serve the roasted lemons and onions and pan drippings in a separate, wide soup plate on a charger.

Stuffed with a seasoned breadcrumb mix, multi-colored roasted cherry tomatoes are a pretty addition and tasty, too.

If you would enjoy a dipping cream, while the bass is roasting prepare cream sauce, scalding two cups of half-and-half cream in a skillet where you have sautéed a very finely chopped white onion in butter.

Sprinkle the sautéed onions with fresh ground pepper, a little, fresh only, chopped mint and a tiny bit of dried thyme and just a pinch of nutmeg. Add a half cup of chopped dry parsley. Salt only after the onions are cooked.

You don't want the butter to brown and you want the onions only *al dente*. Deglaze the skillet with a half cup of Winzertanz and reduce until there is only a tablespoon of liquid in the skillet with the onions.

Add the cream and scald. Allow it to rise and fall three times to thicken. Reserve the cream with the finely chopped onions, in a gravy boat, for those who would enjoy. Place a small ladle on the boat saucer.

By the way, this onion cream keeps beautifully in the fridge in a covered glass container for several days. Can be used in many ways. Great addition to savory crepes or omelets, too.

Chinese Shrimp Batter

2 whole eggs
2 cs bottled water
¼ teaspoon baking soda
3 teaspoons baking powder
1 teaspoon white sugar
3 cups flour
(Note: no salt)

In a small bowl or cup, gently whisk the eggs and water together. Put all the other ingredients into a large bowl. Add the eggs/water mix to the dry ingredients using a fork.

Let the batter rest briefly. This batter works wonderfully with many things, deep-fried in 350 F oil. See my other deep-fry recipes.

Any of this group of fish dish recipes pairs beautifully with any other meal…

French Onion Soup ~ English Style

Sauté in unsalted butter, four cups of uniformly horizontally sliced onions until they are just barely *al dente*. Sprinkle with crushed dry thyme and a pinch of nutmeg, salt and fresh ground pepper and a generous bay leaf. Stir in a quarter teaspoon golden brown sugar (not more, because you don't want sweet soup); the sugar is just meant to enhance the natural sweetness of the onions, and add just a little drop of good maple syrup (try substituting my Asbach Uralt brandy figgy marinating jus).

Deglaze the skillet with a half cup of Asbach Uralt cognac or a very good Sauvignon Blanc; you could even use port for a totally different taste. For something a little different, deglaze the skillet using beer; Belgian Stella Artois or Molson Export Ale works. For me, I prefer to deglaze using the cognac, and just when nearly ready to serve, add a tablespoon of port.

Add four cups of homemade strong full-flavored beef broth, ideally a consommé made from beef bones browned, seared, then roasted in the oven with vegetables and a small piece of whole garlic (it will poach in the broth), and reduce the broth to strengthen the flavor. Strain the broth and clean it the typical way you make consommé, with egg shells or egg whites.

You could strain the broth through clean, never used, cheesecloth, using a sieve and remove the bay leaf. Adjust salt and pepper. Stir in a tablespoon of my Italian blue plum German conserve, mixed with mashed macerated, marinated in brandy black mission figs, or use your favorite gourmet store brand. For something totally different, instead of the conserve, stir in a tablespoon of homemade kumquat marmalade.

Serve with little fresh, crisp, crostini paddles as dippers, open-face, smeared with a little roasted garlic puree, or rub with raw garlic, broiled with fresh Parmesan cheese grated over top. Try putting a slice of mozzarella cheese on the crostini, sprinkled with finely grated dry Parmesan granules, and broil. Very yum!

It's the best French onion soup (English style), ever…you will repeat this recipe often. This soup keeps well for a day or two refrigerated, in a covered glass or stainless-steel container and can be frozen. If you freeze it, separate the onions from the broth in an airtight container, or they will get water-logged as they thaw. Add back the frozen onions to the hot broth just before serving.

Alternate: Strain the onions out of the broth and pulse the onions in your kitchen machine. Add back the broth. Scald two cups of half-and-half cream. Let the cream rise and fall three times to reduce nicely. Gently whisk the onion thickened broth into the hot cream.

Excellent French onion soup, English style, as a cream of onion soup. Really quite special.

For either version: Place a thin slice of mozzarella cheese on top of the cold onion soup. Cut a frozen puff pastry round, about a generous inch larger than the serving bowl width. Sprinkle the pastry with crushed fresh thyme leaves, a little salt and pepper. Paint the outer round edge of the puff pastry with egg wash.

Tip the pastry round over top of each soup bowl at room temperature. Pat the extra egg washed edge tight up against the outside edge of the bowl. Brush the pastry soup-cover with slightly beaten egg yolk.

You might want to refrigerate the pastry covered bowls briefly to protect the puff pastry. (It's made with butter. Don't let the pastry get warm.) Place the pastry covered oven-proof soup bowls on a cookie sheet that has a rim, in a very hot preheated oven at 400 F, until the pastry puffs and takes on a golden color. The pastry will puff in about eight minutes. Serve immediately, very hot.

You can make the soup ahead of time, refrigerate and just add the cheese and the pastry and bake it when you are ready to eat it. Put your under-soup bowl plate on a big charger plate with a paper doily under the bowl. An amazing presentation with the puffed pastry high above the bowl. We first eat with our eyes and it adds to the taste. When ready to enjoy, pierce the puff pastry with a large, round soup spoon, and listen for the compliments.

White Tomato Bruschetta

White tomato bruschetta (or yellow tomato) on grilled black olive bread, with goat cheese and several variables. Another great "Realtor on the run" treat.

A trip to the farmers' market or to your own personal garden (or even to your balcony tomato plant pot) will produce the best of the fresh of the season. Cut an 'x' in the bottom of each tomato skin. In briskly boiling water, using a long-handled spider spoon, blanch the tomatoes for just a few seconds. Or using a long-handled twin-tine fork like the one in your turkey carving set, remove each tomato and place in a water bath metal bowl filled with ice cubes. The metal bowl will help keep the water cold. In just seconds, the skins will slip right off.

Scoop out the seeds and remove the tomato handle core. Coarsely but evenly, chop a medium size Spanish onion.

Zest a large lime. Then using a sharp knife, carefully peel it, removing all the pith. Using a small serrated grapefruit knife, remove the lime segments between each membrane, one by one, and add to a kitchen machine. Crush a fresh clove of garlic or squeeze a little thyme roasted garlic purée into the tomato mix. Add plenty of fresh ground pepper. Add salt and a heaping teaspoon of sugar.

Drizzle in a little oil from your leftover Celebrity goat cheese marinating jar, using a small tea strainer to catch the bay leaves. Spoon out a few goat cheese crumbles from the bottom of the jar.

Add a heaping teaspoon of Wildly Delicious White Truffle Dijon Mustard, and just a spritz of Maplewood Smoked Sunflower and Grapeseed oil, and a generous drop of Black Magic Balsamic vinegar.

Add a half cup of fresh, coarsely chopped parsley and a tablespoon of crushed fresh thyme. Pulse quickly.

Add a couple of finely chopped macerated, marinated fresh black mission figs from your Asbach Uralt cognac jar. Stir in a tablespoon of brandy figgy jus.

Let rest in the fridge while you grill the olive bread or baguette. Split a whole baguette lengthwise or cut bread loaf slices on the diagonal. Brush with oil from your goat cheese marinating jar and using a pastry brush, wipe the bread with just a little smear of roasted garlic purée (a staple in your pantry oil jar).

Use your barbecue upper rack or your kitchen grill or stove broiler to let the bread get just a little crunchy; if using the oven, put the black-olive bread on a metal cookie sheet.

When ready to serve, top the grilled black olive bread with loads of the cold white tomato mix. Add a piece of oil-packed sun-dried red tomato and a Celebrity goat cheese marinated puck, strategically placed so each serving has a piece of cheese.

Return the bread to the very hot grill or top rack stove broiler, just until the cheese starts to melt. Remove the steaming-hot bread and quickly sprinkle with salt and large pieces of coarsely chopped fresh basil leaves, as you are about to serve. Tomatoes love basil.

In addition, for another gourmet touch, add chopped artichoke hearts packed in oil. Sprinkle with fresh grated pepper, just before adding the fresh picked basil.

If you want a totally different bruschetta experience, make a crostini; top the black olive bread with my lobster tails salad recipe, <u>Dine in Tails: Lobster Tails in White Truffle Mustard Homemade Mayo Sauce.</u> Sprinkle with crumbles of goat cheese and drizzle with the goat cheese marinating oil.

And another special bruschetta: Top pre-baked frozen puff pastry squares with the tomato mix and return to a very hot oven just long enough to melt the cheese. Then add fresh basil and serve.

You might find this tomato mix a wonderful opportunity to use those odd-looking "heirloom" tomatoes that are available in mixed colors. Enjoy often!

And then: Have you ever heard of fresh firm peach bruschetta? Simply replace the tomatoes, using very firm, juicy fresh-picked peaches, in peach season. Try the wonderful, white peaches for a spectacular, different, white bruschetta treat. Sprinkle with a little golden-brown sugar, or a drizzle of figgy *jus* from your brandy marinating jar. Top with paper thin slices of prosciutto and marinated goat cheese pucks.

You could choose from many fresh fruits such as juicy Italian blue plums, juicy firm Black Mission figs, marinated in brandy or plain. For pear lovers, choose firm Bosc pears. Top with basil and goat cheese or substitute rocket (watercress) or even pea-greens, just when ready to serve.

Tomato Butter (Jam)—Lady Ralston's Version

Try this recipe for something unusual and discover just how absolutely wonderful it is. Use ripe, green beefsteak tomatoes. Or use white tomatoes, yellow tomatoes or even the newer seed, purple tomatoes. I don't recommend using Heirloom tomatoes in this recipe.

10 pounds of tomatoes (red ones). I prefer beefsteak tomatoes
2 cups white vinegar
½ cup white balsamic vinegar
7 cups of white sugar
1 tablespoon table salt
1 tablespoon ground cloves
1 teaspoon cayenne pepper
1 tablespoon cinnamon

Wash the tomatoes and remove the husk and any black rot spots. Split large tomatoes in half or quarters. Put tomatoes and vinegar(s) into a very large pot and cook down until half of the liquid is evaporated. This will take up to three hours as you will have brought the pot to a boil and then turned it down to simmer. Leave the lid off and stir occasionally using a wooden spoon. Make sure the mixture doesn't stick or burn on the bottom of the pot.

Add the sugar and the spices and simmer another half hour. Important: Pack in hot sterilized glass jars, filled to the top. Allow to cool completely, tented with a clean dish towel and then put lids in position and close tightly. I like to fold a piece of wax paper over top. Store in a cool, dark place. This recipe makes enough to fill three one-pound glass peanut butter jars, or nine or ten small jars. Only pack in glass due to the acid content.

If you have not made tomato butter before, you will want to try this recipe. It's so simple to make and I cannot think of a better way to describe it than to say it is plain old-fashioned delicious as a fondue accompaniment to beef. It is also good with cold sliced beef, veal, seafood and poultry.

Refer to my Sun-dried Tomato Tortillas, using the leftover roast beef filling. It's magically enhanced with this tomato butter.

Another terrific way to use my tomato butter: Make your favorite crepe batter. Instead of using your regular crepe size pan, melt butter in a large shallow skillet, perhaps 12–14 inches in diameter.

Pour just enough crepe batter to barely cover the entire surface into the hot but not browned butter in the skillet. You are making a very thin, very large crepe. Cook on one side until edges release easily and flip or turn using a wide flexible egg turner. Or use your fingers to turn the crepe. Cook the reverse side for just seconds.

As an entree filling, use room temperature medium rare roast beef, carved paper-thin, nearly shredded.

Mound the thin roast beef in a row, like a sausage, in the center of the crepe. Sprinkle just a tiny bit of horseradish cream on the beef. If you don't care for horseradish, as an alternate suggestion: Drizzle just a little of my warm blue cheese dressing over the beef. Beef loves blue cheese. Roll the filled crepe loosely into a large log roll shape.

Cut the roast beef filled crepe into three equal portions, using a very sharp steak knife, cutting on the diagonal. Alongside the crepe, serve a generous dollop of my red beefsteak tomato butter.

Make several crepes in this way to transport to a friend's pot luck. Remember to take along a jar of my tomato butter to enhance the gourmet crepe. And an extra small jar as a hostess gift. A memorable addition to your pot luck takes-along.

My modified tomato butter that I share with you is my creation using as a base, a recipe shared with me more than 35 years ago. I cannot express how wonderful my tomato butter turns out year after year. (Don't forget to try the green beefsteak tomato version.)

A great pairing with this medium rare roast beef filled crepe dish is my chilled favorite sparkling pink Royal de Neuville from France (champagne), in all seasons.

To fill out your meal, a great salad accompaniment is my Boston Bibb lettuce salad with warm blue cheese dressing. All the flavors marry well.

A Special Shellfish Treat

Whether you are celebrating or just making a special family meal, if you enjoy shellfish, you will put my recipes on your keeper-list.

Not everyone eats shellfish, but as a choice at a special brunch it is often welcome. But there's a secret to be insisted upon: The recipes absolutely must be prepared properly. There's no in-between. It's simply not acceptable and can be dangerous if not cooked perfectly.

You will want to advise ahead of time that this is a shellfish special event. Whether you are celebrating or just making a special family meal, if you enjoy shellfish, you will put my recipes on your keeper-list, along with "Dine in" lobster tails.

Present a beautiful table. Remember, first we eat with our eyes, then our other senses awaken.

Coquilles St. Jacques Winzertanz

1-pound sea scallops (rinsed gently in cold running water; not bay scallops)
10 or 12 generous white button mushrooms
1 green onion chopped very fine
1 bay leaf
1 teaspoon parsley, chopped fine
½ cup Winzertanz white German wine; this wine has a little tang, and that works well
Salt, pepper and dried thyme (not the granular one that looks like table pepper)
Unsalted butter
½ teaspoon fresh squeezed lemon juice
homemade (only) chicken stock (enough to make 2 cups when added to broth)
Flour

Butter

Half and half cream

Breadcrumbs (freshly made from plain white bread or French stick)

Grated old or medium Canadian cheddar cheese (not mild)

In a heavy saucepan, sauté the quartered mushrooms in unsalted butter, just once over lightly in a hot pan to sear them; do not overcook, or they will get rubbery. You want the mushrooms still firm to the bite test. Do not add salt yet, because this causes the mushrooms to weep. To the cooked mushrooms, add the rinsed scallops, green onion, bay leaf, parsley, wine and lemon juice.

Bring to a soft boil and reduce heat immediately. Now add seasonings. Simmer for about seven or eight minutes, cover and let stand for a couple of minutes to let the flavors marry. With a slotted spoon, remove just the scallops.

In a small saucepan, make a roux using equal parts butter and flour (five tablespoons each will do nicely); do not brown (watch closely, stirring constantly ideally with a wooden spoon); add to this the liquid left from the scallops and enough chicken stock to make two cups liquid, including one cup half and half cream, stirring well to combine. Add the scallops you removed with the slotted spoon and adjust seasoning if necessary. Scoop the mixture in thickened sauce on to the shells and top with homemade fresh bread crumbs (coarse) and grated cheese.

Place under the preheated broiler, on the top oven rack, until the top starts to turn golden brown. Watch carefully. Do not turn your back on the broiler. Makes eight filled shells.

I started making this dish in the '70s. It is a combination of several recipes I found and modified until I got it to be how I wanted it. I reprinted this in my newspaper cooking column and have since continued to modify it.

This recipe is so rich it really is a "meal," and served with any of my spinach recipes will be most enjoyable if you feel the need to make a bigger entrée. I prefer to serve the Coquilles St. Jacques as a "course" on its own, followed or preceded by vegetables or salad. If you still want a larger course, start with one of my bisques. I have a nice seafood bisque and even a lobster one, and several others to choose from.

If you are fortunate enough to be able to find Royal de Neuville rosé (often available in Quebec, a sparkling champagne-like wine that cannot be called champagne because it does not come from the actual Champagne area in France), try your favorite champagne with your Coquilles St. Jacques. The bubbly cuts the richness of this dish and almost acts as a palate cleanser. If you have leftovers in the pot, refrigerate it immediately. This recipe needs special care after it is made; it can go "off" easily, especially if made in hot humid weather. Don't take chances with seafood. You want to enjoy it.

If you feel the need for a must-have dessert, a plain freshly made panna cotta fills the need. Serve it in a puddle of "reduced" sparkling rose, or reduced champagne, with a sprig of thyme on the side to decorate and an artfully positioned brandy marinated fig, split in half to show its innards. It marries well with the seafood.

Although this is always a "special occasion dish" worthy of a major celebration, treat yourself to this delight often. Everyone will think you spent the whole day in the kitchen. This is one of my recipes for busy people who think they don't have time to cook. Surprise yourself. You can't do much wrong with this dish, so long as you don't turn away from the stove.

An Additional Special Treat for The Coquilles

Cut squares of frozen real butter, puff pastry. Paint each pastry topper with warm compound butter. Top the filled St Jacques coquilles shells with the puff pastry squares. Tuck edges under the shells just a little so the filling can't escape. Paint the pastry with egg wash.

Sprinkle each top with very fine chopped fresh herbs, your choice.

Arrange the shells on a rimmed cookie sheet, lined with a sheet of parchment. Bake until the pastry is just beautifully golden, because the filling is already cooked.

Lobster Waldorf ~ Like No Other

Cross-cut shred romaine lettuce, iceberg lettuce, Boston bibb lettuce, (roll leaves and chiffonade), baby frisée lettuce, cored and coarsely chopped. Toss in baby spinach leaves.

Shred a cup of Sartori BellaVitano brand raspberry ale cheese over the greens. Add a cup of crumbled Celebrity brand Canadian creamy goat cheese pucks from your marinade jar.

Shred a full cup of lobster claw meat (you can buy whole packages of just claw meat), perhaps using two forks, and chop two cups of poached lobster tails. Mound on top of the greens.

From your pantry storage jar, add a cup of candied walnuts. Add a cup of minced candied citrus rind from your pantry sugar jar.

Next, coarsely chop a cup of Asbach cognac marinated black mission figs from your marinating jar and add to the greens.

Just when ready to serve, drizzle with Mazola Corn Oil vinaigrette; equal parts oil, white balsamic vinegar, married with white truffle Dijon by Petite Maison, salt, pepper and a tablespoon of figgy jus from your black mission fig Asbach cognac marinating jar.

Grind fresh peppercorns and sprinkle your favorite sea salt.

Toss and serve in a very large punch bowl.

This salad is wonderful and perhaps a great choice for a wedding or anniversary brunch.

Pair it with my all-time favorite, chilled crackling rosé champagne, Royal de Neuville.

Sweet Lobster Lunch

Gourmet delightful inexpensive lunch. Sweet lobster lunch—small tails—frozen, thawed—steamed over chicken broth. Add a couple of whole garlic cloves and mash them in the sauce later if you like. Remove the meat from the shells.

Melt butter in a skillet. Add the warmed lobster pieces and flambé in very good European brandy/cognac—I use Asbach Uralt. Remove the lobster.

Reduce juices, add cream and scald to thicken. Stir in soft garlic; mashed. Reintroduce lobster and cracked black pepper. The meat is almost sweet. Serve in a warmed shrimp cocktail glass. Really yum.

This is also great filler for crepes. Just make sure the sauce is thickened. You can use as much or as little lobster meat as you like. You can even buy precooked lobster and just gently reheat in butter and flambé. Drizzle with a little figgy *jus* from your cognac marinating jar.

Another time I might add gelatin and let it set up in individual small molds. Serve on a bibb lettuce leaf.

You can also pulse the cooked lobster, add a tiny bit of cream, a sprig of thyme and fresh basil. Rough chop in the blender and make blini. Serve with tiny dollop of sour cream.

Add to Your Lobster Repertoire

Coarsely chop frozen tinned lobster (it is flash frozen on site and a very good product usually). Chop a bit of green onion and a matching amount of chopped fresh celery with leaves. Mix in a little of my lobster oil mayo, a little salt and fresh ground pepper, and top with a smidgeon of shredded tarragon and crispy leaf iceberg lettuce. When ready to serve, drizzle with my cognac Black Mission fig jus. Pack a small Parker House-type soft roll very full of the lobster filling.

Or, serve on a blini or fill a crepe with this mix and serve the crepe in a puddle of reduced cognac jus, mixed with a little maple syrup.

Pork Loin Medallions and Pork Loin Escallops

This all happens in just minutes and like with a minute-steak, cooks very quickly. Don't leave the stove.

Marinate a pork loin in my bell pepper marinade.

Sprinkle with crushed dry fresh thyme leaves. Sprinkle with salt and add lots of fresh ground pepper.

Just before it's ready to sauté, use a thin sharp knife to cut the pork loin in half. Then cut each half in half again. Keep cutting until you have made all the medallions equal in size. Toss the individual medallions in the marinating liquid again, just quickly, and using a spider spoon, remove the medallions and slide them into a very hot sauté skillet with low sides.

Listen for the sizzle. The skillet needs to be very hot but adjust it so the pork doesn't burn. Don't touch for a few minutes as the loin pieces sear. Absolutely do not overcook. When they don't stick to the pan surface, using an egg turner, move the medallion pieces around the skillet, tumbling them so all sides come in contact with the pan surface.

This all happens in just minutes and like with a minute-steak, cooks very quickly. Don't leave the stove.

Empty the skillet that has a slightly browned surface and add a large dollop of butter. Toss quartered white, fresh, firm, button mushrooms (I use about two cups) just to sear once over lightly in the very hot sizzling butter. Add a half teaspoon of fresh dried, crushed thyme. Lots of salt and fresh ground pepper, only after the mushrooms have seared.

Add the mushrooms to the pork loin medallions bowl and toss.

There should be only a smear of butter in the pan. Use it to sauté a half small onion, chopped very fine. Keep the onion moving and turn the burner to low.

Leaving the onion in the skillet, deglaze the very hot pan with about a cup of half-and-half cream. Scald the cream, and using a wooden spoon, move the onions around. Let the cream rise and fall, lower the heat and reduce about a third.

Into the thickened onion cream, stir a heaping tablespoon of Petite Maison White Truffle Mustard. Again, using your wooden spoon, mix well. Then stir in just a teaspoon of Wildly Delicious Black Maple Magic balsamic vinegar. Combine.

Turn the waiting sautéed pork medallion pieces and mushrooms, including the collected liquid, into the white truffle cream sauce. Sprinkle with a little more crushed thyme and add finely chopped parsley (dry will work). Use quite a bit, at least a quarter cup. Cover and let the flavors marry. Adjust seasoning again.

Now add one or two sliced fresh peaches. If fresh peaches are not available, use tinned peaches (not the juice). Add lots of pepper. Peaches love pepper. Stir just once to mix.

Cover and serve over plain buttered basmati rice. A wonderful combination.

Pair this dish with Winzertanz, from the Rhineland, my all-time favorite white wine. Gourmet never tasted so good. Takes no time to prepare and can be made ahead but use within a couple of hours. For some reason, this sort of dish changes its chemistry after being refrigerated and is best served freshly made.

And another way to serve: Prepare wide egg noodles, store-bought or fresh homemade. Drain well and stir melted butter with fresh chiffonade of basil into the pasta. Another day: Serve with fresh-made (instantly cooked) spätzle. Mound with the white truffle mustard pork loin medallions mix.

Alternate: Drain two tins of Bing cherries, packed in their own juice; do not use the juice. Save the juice for another recipe. Stir the cherries into the mustard sauce instead of using peaches.

For a special gourmet treat, marinate the Bing cherries overnight in Asbach Uralt brandy. Using a small spider spoon, lift out the brandied cherries and sprinkle with a pinch of ground cloves, a pinch of nutmeg and a pinch of allspice, a tiny bit of cinnamon. Stir the cherries into the mustard sauce. This cherry sauce is also good served on a crown roast of lamb, roasted duck breast, even on a roasted stuffed turkey breast (one of my all-time ways to prepare turkey); my recipe that never grows old.

Pork Loin Escallops in Marsala Cream Sauce

Remove the silver skin on a generous but not large pork loin, using a very thin sharp knife point and push the knife away from you. Remove it all. Don't miss any, because the silver skin will cause the meat to curl when you sauté it.

Between two sheets of plastic wrap, gently pound and push to stretch the pork medallions. Remove plastic wrap and season the pork loin pieces with salt, pepper, a little thyme and a pinch of nutmeg. Sprinkle the pork with a little dry poultry seasoning.

In a hot skillet with just a little butter, sauté the pork loin medallions and turn only once. Do not overcook. These escallops are fork tender and easily overcooked. Remove from the skillet and rest while you make the sauce.

Deglaze the skillet with a cup of Marsala wine. Let the alcohol burn off, scraping the tiny bits of stuck-on meat. Reduce the wine. It will naturally thicken on medium-high heat. Stir in a quarter cup of your figgy jus from your Asbach Uralt marinating jar. Mash a couple of macerated, brandy marinated black mission figs and add to the sauce. To the very hot sauce, stir in a half cup of half-and-half cream. Remove the sauce from the heat and add a tiny bit of crushed, chopped very fine, fresh sage leaf. Fresh sage is very powerful, so only use a little or it will overtake other flavors.

To add an additional gourmet touch, sear (just once over lightly) tiny, white button mushrooms in very hot but not brown butter, with just a pinch of fresh thyme, then salt and pepper when you remove the mushrooms from the skillet. Stir the mushrooms into the hot Marsala cream sauce and drizzle the sauce over the escallops.

Serve with homemade pappardelle pasta or cut sheets of store-bought fresh lasagna noodles into wide strips and simmer al dente in gently boiling water. Salt and pepper. Remember, homemade pasta cooks very quickly. Enjoy! So yum!

Christmas Cake

Christmas cake is outrageous—you can enjoy it all year long because some cakes keep for ages. Here are some tasty Christmas desert ideas. And a little something extra:

Espresso Cheesecake (Or Tiramisu Cheesecake)

Filling:
9–130-gram (4.5 oz) heat sealed packaged logs of Celebrity label goat cream cheese
5 whole eggs plus 2 yolks
¼ teaspoon vanilla
¼ teaspoon salt
1¾ cup granulated sugar
4 tablespoons all-purpose flour
½ cup full fat whipping cream
2 tablespoons of cold extra strong espresso coffee
1 tablespoon of Asbach Uralt brandy

Basic pastry:

1 cup unsalted butter
½ cup sugar
2 egg yolks
½ teaspoon vanilla
2 cups flour

With a pastry cutter, work together the butter and sugar and egg yolks. Add flour until the mixture reaches the consistency of coarse cornmeal.

Pat two-thirds of the mixture with your hand into the bottom of 30 cm ungreased spring form pan and bake in a preheated 400 F oven until just golden (not brown)—about seven minutes. You will have to watch this closely the first few times until you see how the mixture reacts to your oven.

Remove and let it cool until you can touch the metal pan. (I stick the pan in freezer for a few minutes).

With the remaining pastry, pat to form the side crust nearly to the top edge of the pan, overlapping, slightly, the cooked pastry. The side pastry will bake with the filling.

Into a large mixing bowl, put five packages of Celebrity label Canadian goat cream cheese, which is at room temperature, and has been broken in several pieces each, to take the strain off your mixer motor.

Add the eggs and extra yolks and beat until the mixture is creamy, increasing speed as the mixture allows. Add sugar, vanilla, salt and flour and continue beating, starting on low speed and increasing speed as flour is mixed into the batter.

Now add liquid cream and the espresso coffee along with the brandy and beat a further five minutes. After adding a full cup of grated Sartori BellaVitano Espresso cheese, mix on low speed only until the grated cheese is just incorporated.

Turn it into the waiting pastry shell and bake for 15 minutes at 400 F, then turn the oven down to 325 F and continue baking for about one hour, longer if necessary. Bake on the bottom rack of your oven. This cake is very dense, not unlike a fruitcake, and is baked on the bottom rack.

Check the center by inserting a sharp knife. When the knife comes out clean, the cake is ready to remove from the oven.

When the pan is cool enough to touch, you will see that the pastry has a tiny air space between the pastry and the pan. Slide a sharp off-center spatula around the pan in the air space to disconnect any tiny pieces of pastry that might be stuck. Release the spring form pan lock and gently lift the ring off the cheesecake. Leave the cake on the pan base.

If you like, decorate with the remaining whipping cream that has been whipped quite stiff, with three tablespoons of icing sugar, a drizzle of brandy, a teaspoon of figgy jus from your black mission fig marinating jar if you have it, and ½ teaspoon vanilla.

Put the stiff whipped cream into a forcing bag and squirt an edge all around the cake. If you want to make your cheesecake look even more elegant, decorate the top with the cream and a few shards of Sartori BellaVitano Espresso cheese, in the center, along with thin shards of white chocolate. Or sprinkle with grated rock-hard white chocolate. Top with a few paper-thin rinds from your citrus candied peel pantry sugar jar.

I hope you enjoy making this wonderful recipe as much as I do. You are sure to receive many compliments from your family and friends. (You may even have to hide the cake—that is, if there is any left).

If you are appointed to bring dessert to a pot luck dinner, pot luck will never be the same. Note this recipe makes a very large cheesecake and it will keep, covered, in the refrigerator for a few days. It "sets up" beautifully. Serve in small wedges because it is beyond rich, but very wonderful.

Alternate: Fruit-enhanced cheesecake, a light, enjoyable treat that is a keeper for sure.

Prepare pastry. Prepare cheese filling. Put two cups of the cheese mixture onto the baked pastry in the spring form pan.

Then add a fresh firm fruit mix. Here's how to make the fruit ready: In a large stainless-steel skillet, put thick slices of firm, fresh, pitted skin removed peaches, fresh blue or yellow Italian plums, skins on, and Bosc pears, peeled, cut in equal portions. Add a quarter cup of cold butter.

Allow the fruit to sauté and make its own juices. Lower heat, cover and let the fruit soften slightly.

Add a little sugar simple syrup, and/or a little figgy *jus* from your cognac black mission fig marinating jar. Squeeze a little fresh lemon juice over the fruit. Add five or six whole cloves in a tied cheesecloth sac. You might like to add a sprinkle of nutmeg and cinnamon and/or allspice. Add a pinch of salt.

Flambé the fruit with a full cup of cognac. Burn off the alcohol. Stir in a half cup of port. Let the fruit mix cool in the fridge and the liquid will congeal.

Using a large serving spoon, place the sautéed fruit mix on top of the two cups of the cheese mixture you placed on the baked pastry. Then top with the remaining cheese mixture.

Bake the cheesecake on the oven bottom rack until a knife inserted in the cheesecake comes out clean. Set your timer for 40 minutes and check periodically.

Alternate: Sauté firm, fresh, marinated but not macerated black mission figs, and proceed the same as with mixed fruits.

For another opportunity to make a very special cheesecake, use my cooked down mix of figgy sauce made with macerated, marinated in Asbach Uralt brandy black mission figs and my German plum conserve, made with Italian blue plums in season.

The result in all choices is very tasty for sure. And quite likely a cheesecake you have never enjoyed before.

This recipe makes a very large cheesecake that keeps well in the refrigerator for several days. So, if you are preparing for a dinner party, you can easily make your cake a day in advance. Store in the refrigerator in a covered container large enough to accommodate the size of the spring form pan base.

Pre-cut into manageable small size wedges, because it is very filling. Ideal after a light meal rather than a heavy one. Or served alone with a special coffee such as Asbach Rudesheimer, a few hours after a formal dinner settles.

Another Alternate: This is the base recipe from the mid-1970s, from which I developed all the variables for my other cheesecake recipes.

Pineapple Cheesecake

Filling:

5–8 oz. pkg cream cheese
5 eggs plus 2 yolks
¼ teaspoon vanilla
¼ teaspoon salt
1¾ cup sugar
3 tablespoon flour
½ cup whipping cream

1 20 oz. tin crushed pineapple (drained) packed in light sugar syrup. (It's important to use pineapple packed in light sugar syrup; most tins are packed just in juice or water). If necessary, drain the tin of pineapple and save the juice. Stir a matching amount of liquid into the pineapple by replacing the liquid with homemade light sugar syrup; equal parts sugar and water simmered until the sugar melts into the water. This is important for the end texture of the baked cake.

Basic pastry:

1 cup (sweet only) butter
½ cup sugar
2 egg yolks
½ teaspoon vanilla
2 cup flour

With a pastry cutter, work together the butter and sugar and egg yolks. Add flour until the mixture reaches the consistency of coarse cornmeal.

Pat two-thirds of the mixture with your hand into the bottom of a 30-cm ungreased spring form pan and bake in preheated 400 F oven until just golden (not brown)—about seven minutes. You will have to watch this closely the first few times until you see how the mixture reacts to your oven.

Remove and let cool until you can touch the metal pan. (I stick the pan in the freezer for a few minutes).

With the remaining pastry, pat it to form a side crust nearly to the top edge of pan, overlapping slightly the cooked pastry. The side pastry will bake with the filling.

Into a large mixing bowl, put five packages of cream cheese, which is at room temperature and has been broken in several pieces each to take the strain off your mixer motor. Add the eggs and extra yolks and beat until mixture is creamy, increasing speed as mixture allows. Add sugar, vanilla, salt and flour and continue beating, starting on low speed and increasing speed as the flour is mixed into batter.

Now add liquid cream and beat a further five minutes. After adding pineapple, mix on low speed only until the pineapple is incorporated.

Turn into the waiting pastry shell and bake for 15 minutes at 400 F, then turn the oven down to 325 F and continue baking for about an hour, longer if necessary.

Check the center by inserting a sharp knife. When it comes out clean, the cake is ready to remove from the oven.

If you like, decorate it with the remaining whipping cream that has been whipped with three tablespoons of icing sugar and a ½ teaspoon vanilla.

Put cream into a forcing bag and squirt an edge all around cake. If you want to make your cheesecake look even more elegant, decorate the top with the cream and a few pieces of pineapple in the center.

And then there's the not-so-typical, my dark fruit cake, in the Christmas fashion:

Lady Ralston's Dark Fruitcake

This not only makes a wonderful Christmas fruitcake, but is great for weddings too. The recipe is my own combination of a mixture my mother used, one from her sister-in-law and a few variations I've made over the years. It is truly one of the best I've ever eaten.

1-pound unsalted butter

2 cup fine white sugar

1½ cup light brown sugar

6 eggs

1 cup milk

1 cup strong fresh-brewed coffee (definitely not instant coffee)

4 tablespoon mixed spices (cinnamon, allspice, cloves, mace, nutmeg, cardamom)

1 tablespoon soda (mixed with milk)

2 pounds Raisins (sultana)

2 pounds Currants

½ pound shelled walnuts pieces

½ pound mixed citron peel (use from your pantry citrus rind sugar jar)

1 cup homemade strawberry jam

½ pound chopped candied mixed fruit

½ pound candied red maraschino cherries

½ pound candied green maraschino cherries

1 teaspoon salt

½ cup Marsala wine

4½-5 cup flour

Cream butter and sugars. Add beaten eggs, coffee, spices and milk. In a large bowl (or pot) mix all the fruit and nuts with as much of the flour as you need to dredge them.

Back to the batter, stir in the strawberry jam, salt and add to fruit. Mix in the leftover flour.

Mix very well and the spoon mixture into two 10-inch spring form pans lined with greased brown paper. Bake at 325 F for about two and a half hours. Watch closely in the last half hour.

Let stand for about 10 minutes, invert and remove the brown paper. Wrap cakes in cheesecloth soaked in Marsala wine and store in an airtight container. This will keep for many months. That's why I always made my Christmas cake in August.

If you wish, when the cakes are about a week old, cover the top with almond paste and regular white icing. Re-wrap and store. The recipe makes about 12 pounds of cake.

And of course, some people prefer a light Christmas fruitcake, and enjoyed this recipe initially published in the mid-1970s.

Light Fruitcake

Although dark fruitcake is customarily frosted in one form or another, light fruitcake seldom is. If you have never attempted to bake a fruitcake before, start with the light one. There is very little labor involved; just allow yourself plenty of time for your oven to do its job. Wrap your fruitcake in several layers of cheesecloth that has been soaked in your favorite brandy. For an unusual, but pleasant new flavor in an old method, swap Southern Comfort for the brandy.

Store in an airtight container for the next six or seven weeks and you'll have a delightful treat to offer guests who will pop in for the first taste of Christmas at your house.

Remember not to peek, as this causes your oven to drop at least 25 degrees. When it is nearly time for your baking to be finished, then and only then, test for doneness.

Don't be overly worried if your baking requires an extra 10 minutes or so. Every oven performs differently, and manufacturers guarantee controls only to a 25-degree accuracy.

Remember to preheat your oven for at least half an hour before you use it, as this allows time for the heat to stabilize.

Pineapple Fruitcake (Light)

¾ cup butter
1 cup white sugar
½ teaspoon salt
2 eggs. well beaten
3 cup flour
2 teaspoon baking powder
½ pound white raisins
½ pound candied red cherries
½ pound candied red and green pineapple
1 med. Tin, crushed pineapple in light sugar syrup (I always used Dole brand.)

Preheat oven to 325 F. Cream butter and sugar. Add salt and eggs. Add 2½ cups of the flour with baking powder. Dredge fruit with remaining flour and add to the cake batter, combining well. Add drained crushed pineapple and stir till thoroughly mixed.

Cut a piece of brown paper; butter a 10-inch-square pan and fit the paper. Turn the paper so the greased side is up. Pour in batter and bake for about 1½ hours. Cool. Remove the paper and allow it to cool completely before wrapping and storing.

And not to be forgotten is my old wonderful German Asbach Stollen, as published many years ago. It's easy to make and is a real show-stopper on your winter banquet or buffet table.

Not being a sweets-preference person, I do enjoy a treat once in a while, although given the option, I would always choose a savory. When I had family, before the empty-nest syndrome and back when I was teaching "Gourmet Cooking with Carolyne," I had all my holiday baking ready for Christmas indulgences by the end of August. I accounted for every minute of my real estate life, but always found time to have a light genoise layer cake on hand (that's what is used to make a spectacular "jelly roll," ready every week for many years) to be filled with my favorite konditerei stiff whipped Chantilly Cream in any flavor that struck my fancy on a given day, sometimes with fresh fruit in season, likely fresh peaches, fresh strawberries or raspberries, placed on the base layer and drizzled with liqueur best suited for a match. I confess, the genoise layer cake, cream filled became my favorite; it is so light and airy, followed closely by my German Asbach Stollen.

REALLY!

Christmas Fruitcake Croutons ~ Yes, Really!

Have you ever thought of cutting thick slices of fruitcake into cubes and roasting them in sizzling sweet homemade oven-roasted garlic purée butter? Sprinkle with salt and pepper while still hot.

You could use either light or dark fruitcake.

Use as a topper for your French Onion Soup ~ English Style, or toss with your favorite mesclun salad, drizzled with 3:1 red wine vinegar and best quality olive oil.

Wickedly wonderful. Really!

You could even make roasted in unsweetened butter, "pound cake croutons" (or even use chocolate pound cake) to serve with your favorite fruit salad or with your Tomato Carpaccio (poke a caper in each crouton when sprinkling over the tomatoes). Spritz with cognac.

"Over the top:" Split slices of barely cooked but crispy fatty bacon strips, and wrap each individual crouton with the thin bacon strips.

Or wrap the pound cake croutons in paper thin strips of very fresh crispy cucumber.

You could put roasted croutons on a party-size skewer and top any salad with a couple of skewers. Or maybe make a pocket of croutons in a lettuce-leaf cup.

A Little Holiday Something, From Me to You

When you set your table for any celebration this year, or at Christmas or whatever festivity you celebrate, here is an idea.

Place a candle in a small holder at each place setting. Do not light the candle. When you are all gathered at the table, have the host or hostess light one candle using the flame from a previously lighted candle in the center of the table (or from the center-piece arrangement).

The host or hostess will then light the candle of the first guest to the right, using the flame from his/her candle, as the guest tips their candle in receipt of the flame being offered.

That guest will do the same for the person to his/her right, until you make the way all the way around the table. As each candle is lighted, say something like, "I give thanks for your friendship" or "I give thanks for your love" or even just, "I'm glad that you are here today." Get creative and enjoy.

The light shining from each candle at each place setting will cast a wonderful glow on each guest's face. After grace or after the first course, you may want to extinguish the candles, one by one, with a small long-handled flame extinguisher cover, passing it counter clockwise around the table, ending with the host/hostess.

May you and yours have a fabulous holiday season and a wonderful new year.

Soup's on! ~ At My House and Yours!

Let's have a "soup-er supper" to close out the year! Here's my special creamy broccoli cheese soup, like no other.

Sauté a half small onion and a generous whole garlic clove, and add a coarsely chopped head of well-washed broccoli. I say well-washed for a reason: One day many years ago, I learned a valuable lesson with a nice fresh store-bought head of broccoli. I cut off the bottom ends of each segment and washed it carefully in an oversize colander, only to discover when I pulled the head apart that there was the most beautiful color-matched caterpillar hiding deep inside.

I never would have seen it, but it moved. I thought I was seeing things. I let the caterpillar finish its lunch by gently tossing the piece out in the garden, with the caterpillar intact.

In the large pot, cover the broccoli with well-seasoned homemade chicken stock, and add two medium-size peeled potatoes, quartered. Add two small whole peeled carrots and one small stick of celery. Salt as you would for boiled potatoes.

Adjust the chicken stock to cover completely. Generously salt and pepper. Add a most tiny sprinkle of poultry seasoning or a quarter teaspoon of fresh chopped sage, (easy on the sage, either way; it's in the poultry seasoning and it can be overpowering); a sprinkle of chopped rosemary and crushed thyme. Add a pinch of fresh, freeze-dried parsley (LightHouse brand is terrific) and just a tiny bit of basil. Finally, add a tablespoon of granulated sugar and a few pieces of your favorite sweet apple.

When the potatoes and other vegetables are fork tender, remove the pot from the fire. When cooled slightly, purée in a blender or kitchen machine. You can package and freeze this base until ready to use.

Note: If I happen to have frozen mirepoix, leftover from some other cooking, I toss it into this soup and continue to simmer briefly, before I purée.

On a day you will use it, thaw the base in the refrigerator and when ready to prepare, scald half and half cream on high heat, 1:3 letting it rise and fall three times to reduce. Add small chunks of cheddar cheese and stir constantly until the cheese melts into the cream. (You don't have to add the cheese; the plain soup is still very good.)

Remove the scalded, reduced cream from the burner. Stir in the broccoli base.

Now for the gourmet touch, just when ready to serve: Add a little congealed figgy jus from your Asbach Uralt cognac marinating jar and drop in a small, finely chopped marinated black mission fig, on top of a dollop of very cold full-fat sour cream.

Another way to serve: Into a hot bowl of soup, top with a dollop of tight full-fat sour cream. Do not stir. Carefully mound on top of the sour cream dollop, a teaspoon of Beet and Red Onion marmalade by Wildly Delicious. The gentle "kick" of the marmalade makes a wonderful mix of flavors, as you enjoy your first spoonful.

A different serving option: [close up]
You could toast diagonally cut slices of black-olive bread or baguette, butter the toasts generously and use as soup dippers. Or you could cut the toasts into crispy croutons and float the crunchy croutons on the soup plates, as you serve.

Or, when ready to serve and the steaming hot creamy soup is being plated, add a puck of your marinated Celebrity label creamy Canadian goat cheese. Do not stir. Drizzle with maple syrup. This delightful mixture of flavors will have you wanting seconds.

In the holiday season, you might like to top the dollop of very cold sour cream with some sweet, gooey, sautéed cranberries. I make a wonderful, very sweet, rhubarb confit and it can be used as a topper, too.

Note: Don't eat the base before adding it to the scalded reduced cream. You might find it tastes awful; on the odd occasion broccoli can be bitter, although served as a vegetable, I have never found it to be. However, once added to the hot reduced cream, it is truly terrific! And any bitterness disappears. Adjust seasoning just before serving. You might want to add a little salt and pepper.

If you love broccoli, you might want to try this very different broccoli soup. With the winter weather upon us, you might want to stock up your freezer with lots of containers of homemade chicken broth, and the base for several easy-to-make and easier-to-enjoy.

Some Great "Pasta-bilities"

Figgy plum gnocchi, pink pasta with pears and bacon, and some green beans on the side.

Figgy Plum Gnocchi in Fruity Bagna Càuda Sauce

Boil four medium floury peeled potatoes, not the waxy type potatoes, in cold salted water, Drain. Let air dry briefly. Rice the cooled, but not cold, potatoes. Ricing keeps the gnocchi light and fluffy, melt in your mouth tender.

Add two whole eggs and a half cup each of regular flour and hazelnut flour. Add a half cup of grated dry cheese. (I like a mix of Romano and Parmesan.) Work the dough just until all ingredients are incorporated. Do not overwork the dough.

Chop two brandied black mission marinated figs that have naturally macerated in the cognac and gently work the chopped figs into the dough. Drizzle just a few drops of your brandy marinating *jus* from the jar into the dough. Knead just briefly.

Chop fine, one very ripe fresh Italian plum. (You can use a frozen plum if you have them. Frozen plums get juicy and sticky sweet as they have released their natural juices.) Work the chopped plum into the dough.

Let mixture rest for 15 minutes.

Pull off pieces of the dough and roll by hand into long skinny sausage-like strips on a large wooden board.

Cut the dough roll into generous bite-size pieces. Have a pot of boiling salted water ready and just simmer the gnocchi until they float (al dente). When gnocchi float to the surface, they are cooked.

Make my bagna càuda sauce, using fresh cream and your favorite cheeses. When the sauce has thickened, stir in two firm chopped, but not minced, marinated black mission figs. Add a fresh juicy chopped Italian blue plum.

Add the poached gnocchi to the bagna càuda sauce just when ready to serve.

Place several gnocchi in a puddle of bagna càuda, in a flat, deep, soup plate that has wide rim sides.

Park a whole firm brandy marinated fig and a half pitted fresh plum on the rim, with a large basil leaf on the side, just when ready to serve.

A flute of Royal de Neuville Sparkling Rose, or your favorite champagne is a good pairing here.

This is an entree dish best served alone, but if you want a salad, serve it after the gnocchi course; the French often serve salad as a final course. And a cheese fruit plate with the salad course closes the stomach.

Alternate 1: Perhaps offer my Hazelnut Watercress Pesto, served in a small dish with a little ladle, for those who might enjoy a drizzle on their gnocchi. The flavors match.

Alternate 2: Flambé sautéed fresh lobster, using Asbach if available, or substitute your favorite cognac, or if no fresh lobster is available, use a large tin of flash frozen lobster, very gently heated and flambéed. In a separate skillet, sauté in butter, a small chopped piece of celery and leaf, with a tiny bit of fresh chopped green onion.

Stir into the bagna càuda sauce.

Break up the lobster pieces and add to the bagna càuda sauce. Serve the hazelnut fruit gnocchi in a puddle of the lobster sauce. When ready to serve, sprinkle with a little shredded fresh tarragon. Enjoy! (If you have made homemade lobster oil, now is a good opportunity to use it; drizzle a little very special lobster oil over each serving. Do not stir.)

St Michael's figgy treats—it's mine...

Using my Stollen dough recipe, prepare to the stage of adding the fruits. Instead, paste a figgy plum mixture on the dough, fold and bake.

The Figgy Filling

Put two cups of black mission figs, marinated in Asbach Uralt, into a stovetop saucepan. Add a cup of my plum conserve or your favorite plum jam.

Bring to a gentle simmer. Stir in a little figgy *jus* from your cognac marinating jar.

From your candied citrus peel sugar pantry jar, chop some orange strands very fine and add to the pot. Squeeze in the juice of a half lemon. Add the juice of a half sweet orange. Stir and let bubble just a little. Let the gooey paste cool to room temperature. Stir in a half cup of chopped candied walnuts. You want to be able to spread the mixture on the dough.

Now if you want to make figgy stuffed cookies, roll out your favorite pastry dough and cut into two long rectangles. Make a figgy sausage shape from the filling. Use plastic wrap and roll and shape the log and refrigerate for an hour.

Position the figgy log on the pastry rectangle and pull the sides of the pastry over the figgy log to wrap. Roll with your fingers and place seam-side down on the cutting board. Chop in pieces the way you would cut gnocchi. Place individual filled pastry pieces on a parchment covered cookie sheet and bake in a medium hot oven, middle rack just until the pastry is cooked. The figgy log is already cooked. Do not over bake. You don't want the figgy filled pastries to dry out.

Alternate: If you would prefer, use fresh Medjool dates, chopped fine, mashed together with my plum conserve.

Pink Pasta with Pears and Bacon...Surprise Sauce is Wonderful!

Equal weight rough chopped cooked beets and "00" pasta-making flour. Add one whole egg. Mix in Cuisinart machine. Let rest in plastic wrap for half hour, at room temperature. Process three times in pasta machine until quite thin. Hang to dry.

While pasta is drying, make sauce. Fry bacon until quite crisp. Remove bacon from pan. In the bacon fat, add butter; sear fresh Bosc pears cut into thick slices, add a half cup of my candied salted large walnut pieces. Add two cups of watercress. Stir in just a tiny bit of oven-roasted garlic purée from your stored refrigerator jar. (Hint: Don't store oven-roasted garlic cloves in oil to prevent mold spores from attacking; the spores can kill. Seriously).

Stir in a quarter cup of brandy figgy marinating jus and one finely chopped fresh black mission fig. Crumple the bacon on top and incorporate.

Squeeze on a bit of fresh lemon. Top with small chunks of room temperature blue cheese just when ready to serve.

In boiling salted water, cook the beet pasta for just one minute. Fresh pasta cooks very quickly. Twirl a serving onto a large dinner plate.

Toss the warm pear sauce over top the hot beet pasta pulled fresh from the boiling water. No need to drain the pasta, just take from the pot, wrapping the pasta around the tines of a large fork. The water attached to the pasta just enhances the sauce. Grind fresh peppercorns, spritz with just a little olive oil and serve.

Some people like to use pesto on all pasta dishes. If that's you, you will want to use my watercress pesto recipe. (add the recipe)

Might seem an odd choice to some, but the fruity tones in French label George's Beaujolais is a nice pairing here.

Remember to let the red wine breathe before you serve the wine in a large bowl-shape glass on a thin stem, with a wide rim, not a tapered bowl (this shape is sometimes referred to as a Chardonnay white wine bowl); you want the Beaujolais to come in contact with the oxygen to enhance the bouquet.

Never fill a large bowl wine glass more than half full; it's ideally best only a third full in such a glass. You can always serve more later.

It's My Gnocchi ~ making It Gourmet Style

Wipe the skins of dry baking potatoes with butter and bake. Split in half and scoop out the skins. Choose large potatoes. They are baked when a knife inserted comes out clean. Do not over-bake as that will change the flesh texture.

At 400 F in a preheated oven, this could take one hour. Check periodically after 45 minutes. Set your timer(s). Your smart phone timer comes in handy, especially if you are multi-tasking.

Cut the potatoes in half and scoop out the flesh into a large bowl. Press through a ricer. It's the only way to get the potatoes to a flour-like consistency. Add salt and pepper and whatever you like into the dough at this point, such as cooked spinach, mashed beets, or really fresh chopped herbs. You could even add a little grated cheese.

For three large potatoes you will need a half cup of flour and one large egg yolk. (Save the whites, never toss them; freeze them in an ice cube tray and reserve the frozen cubes in a plastic bag.) Work the dough with your hands, just gently until the mixture forms a ball. Divide the dough in segments and roll each into a thin long sausage shape using your hands, working on a lightly floured surface.

Using a knife, cut the sausage shape dough into one-inch pieces and tip each piece with the tines of a fork to make little indents to hold your sauce.

Place the gnocchi on a lightly floured cookie sheet, not touching one another. Let the dough air dry in the refrigerator for 10-15 minutes.

Using a spider, tip the gnocchi into a pot of softly boiling cold, salted water. Never use water from the hot water tap. It could contain sediment from the hot water boiler tank. The process is like making spätzle. The gnocchi will float to the surface quickly.

In the meantime, melt a knob of unsalted butter in a sauté skillet. Do not brown the butter unless it is your intention to serve nutty (noisette) flavored gnocchi. But the butter does need to be very hot. Use just enough butter to coat the gnocchi.

Using a spider to remove the gnocchi will allow the liquid to stay in the pot. Place the gnocchi in the hot butter and toss to coat each piece. You might decide to serve the finished gnocchi as is with a sprinkle of grated Sartori BellaVitano Raspberry cheese and chopped fresh basil or parsley.

Or you could add your cooked gnocchi to your favorite tomato sauce or a rose sauce. Or even to an Alfredo sauce.

For a totally different gnocchi experience, just when ready to serve, drizzle each low, wide soup plate with a little brandy figgy jus from your black mission fig marinating jar. You could even chop a couple of the marinated figs and sprinkle over top. Totally gourmet, totally wonderful. See my <u>rose pasta sauce</u> recipe.

Green Beans on the Side

I usually cook green beans, starting them in salted, cold water, bringing them to a boil just until fork tender.

But for this recipe, I boiled the water first in a covered pot. Salt the boiling water. Toss in "Frenched" green beans. Frenched is simply split each green bean, individually, lengthwise, top to bottom, so you have a bowl of green bean strings.

Par boil. Using tongs, remove the quickly cooked green beans and transfer them into a bowl of ice cube filled water. Watch the green color come to life.

In a skillet, in the few minutes it takes to cook the green beans, sauté chopped shallots in hot, but not brown, sizzling butter, just until translucent. Sprinkle with salt, fresh ground peppercorns, and chopped fresh mint. Toss the iced Frenched green beans into the sautéed shallots just to mix and heat through.

Remove and put the mixture into a serving bowl or onto a large platter.

Drizzle with just a bit of my <u>watercress pesto</u> and top with coarsely chopped candied walnuts or candied whole hazelnuts from your pantry jar.

Sprinkle with minced citrus rinds from your panty citrus sugar jar. Sprinkle just a few grains of the citrus sugar from the jar over top, and a sprinkle of salt. Do not toss or stir.

This fresh, crunchy vegetable green bean side can be served with many entrees. Enjoy!

To serve the Frenched green beans as a salad, refrigerate when completed and bring to the patio to serve with your barbecued steak or tender yummy fish cooked in barbecue papillote. You might like to sprinkle the finished salad, just when ready to serve, with hot chili flakes, as much or as little as you prefer.

Rapini Bruschetta, Turkey Breast Stuffing, Apples Gone Puff and More

Here are some handy recipes for entertaining that busy salespeople can make in a hurry with ordinary pantry fare.

Here are some handy recipes for entertaining that busy salespeople can make in a hurry with ordinary pantry fare.

Turkey Breast Stuffing ~ Just A Little Bit Italian

Squeeze out about two pounds of Italian sausage (if you enjoy the really spicy one, that's fine) into a skillet with about a cup of sautéed shallots. Add a pinch of ground cloves and salt, pepper and fresh chopped parsley. Sprinkle with your favorite herbs.

Push the meat mixture around the skillet on medium-high heat, just until sausage loses its pink color.

Add a half cup of my Offley Ruby Port fruit compote. Remove the mixture to a bowl to cool. Deglaze the skillet with a splash of Marsala wine (the fragrance is wonderful) and add the drippings to the meat. Stir in a cup or two of fresh, loose breadcrumbs made from leftover dried black-olive bread, and a half cup of fresh, grated, Sartino BellaVitano raspberry cheese.

Whisk two large eggs and add to the mixture. Use your hands or the paddle for your kitchen machine. Try to keep the mixture loose, rather than too compact.

Cover in a glass, airtight container and refrigerate overnight.

Open the split turkey breast. Brush with duck fat if you have it, otherwise brush with clarified butter. Sprinkle with your favorite herbs and spices.

Fill it with the stuffing, roll and tie it postage style. Roast on the bottom rack, tented with foil, shiny side in, at medium heat 350 F, until the turkey meat is perfectly cooked. Do not overcook. During the last five minutes of roasting, remove the foil and baste with port compote.

Serve with two vegetables such as sautéed rapini, and split in half a roasted acorn squash in its skins served in a separate side dish, with a little brown sugar (alternate to brown sugar: Use a drizzle of marinating jus from your Asbach cognac marinating jar) and butter, along with a ferrous serving of my mashed, whipped potatoes (swirl in a little horseradish cream for an additional gourmet touch, or for a completely different taste, stir in a little Petite Maison white truffle Dijon).

This special Christmas meal will be a regular at your house, even at Thanksgiving or other celebration meals.

If you have extra stuffing, form into generous rolled sausage shapes, place in a pound cake baking pan, cover in foil, shiny side in and bake alongside the turkey breast. Ideal for serving a day later on crostini with my recipe for grilled, roasted bell peppers and onions mix (see my giant meatballs recipe).

This stuffed turkey breast is a great between-the-holidays treat, if guests arrive unexpectedly who were not part of the initial Christmas turkey dinner. It is also a perfect recipe for a buffet service for a take-along to a pot luck event. The host or hostess will be pleased to share your special treat with other guests and will welcome your contribution to any event, large or small.

Rapini Bruschetta

Cut off about an inch of root ends. Blanche fresh rapini in salted cold tap water, brought to a boil. Rapini will wilt much like spinach does. Test a thick stem to be sure the stems are cooked through. Drain thoroughly in a large colander. Push out excess water. Chop fine on a cutting board. Add the rapini back to the hot pot that you have melted unsalted butter in, with a teaspoon of oven roasted garlic purée from your refrigerated jar.

I learned that oven-roasted whole garlic purée will keep for ages in an airtight glass jar and not grow those deadly mold spores if you do not store the purée in oil. Just plain garlic purée, straight from the oven to the fridge. Air-tight.

Mash as much purée as you like into the melted butter and stir in the chopped hot rapini.

Spread toasted, buttered crostini with garlic purée and top with the finely chopped rapini. Crumble Celebrity brand Canadian goat cheese over the rapini and sprinkle with minced sun-dried tomatoes, oil packed.

Alternate for adults: Drizzle with a little congealed figgy *jus* from your black mission fig Asbach brandy marinating jar.

Next time you go to a pot luck, prepare everything ahead of time and assemble when you get to your destination. Many people would be introduced to rapini for the very first time. They might wonder how they missed out on this terrific veggie. Delicious! Leaves a wonderful after-taste on the palate.

Suggestion to take along: Make a mixture of various <u>bruschetta combinations</u> (peaches, anyone?).

Bruschetta is a perfect accompaniment to any baked Italian pasta dish.

Want a whole meal? Serve the wonderful bruschetta selection with a hot bowl of my homemade minestrone soup or my delicious bean soup. Make plenty. Everyone will want an extra or two, maybe three crostini? (I love to make crostini using toasted, buttered, black-olive bread.)

Apples Gone Puff

Peel, core and cut six firm cooking apples into eighths. Sauté apple segments in hot butter. Sprinkle with just a tiny bit of salt. When fork tender, add a half cup of golden-brown sugar and a quarter cup of Canadian maple syrup. Sprinkle with nutmeg, cinnamon and just a most tiny pinch of ground cloves. This should only take about five minutes. Drizzle with a little oil from your Celebrity brand Canadian creamy goat cheese pucks marinating jar. Sprinkle with chopped candied walnuts from your pantry jar. Mince a little citrus rind from your pantry sugar jar and stir in after the apples are soft.

No fresh apples? Keep a few tins of apple pie filling handy in your pantry for when the urge to make this quick treat appears. Sprinkle the pie filling with the nutmeg, cinnamon and cloves, and the maple syrup; drizzle with a little oil from your goat cheese marinating jar.

Bake butter-made frozen puff pastry as per package directions. Cut in square napkins, or using a ring, cut circle shapes of the puff pastry, brush with a little egg wash before baking and line with fresh coarse homemade breadcrumbs to catch any extra liquid (same as you would do making homemade strudel).

Top the baked pastry with a heaping mound of the sautéed apples or apple pie filling.

Crumble a log of Canadian Celebrity label Cinnamon Goat Cheese over the hot sautéed apples, or the apple pie filling, mounded on the pastry, and serve immediately with a hot cup of your favorite coffee.

A nice weekend brunch treat, especially if you are entertaining house guests.

Alternate: Top the hot baked puff pastry with chopped firm marinated black mission figs from your Asbach Uralt brandy jar. Crumble the creamy Canadian goat cheese over top of the figs, while puff pastry is still hot from the oven. Sprinkle with candied minced citrus rinds and slivered pistachio nuts.

Special 'Pigs in A Different Blanket'

Squeeze out the innards of your favorite raw sausage. About four cups. Mix with sautéed minced onion, garlic (you could use your pantry oven-roasted garlic purée, loads if you love it), and your favorite herbs and spices. You could mince a little sun-dried tomato packed in oil and add to the meat mix. Add just a little grated orange zest.

Let cool enough to handle. Shape into sausage shapes. For something a little different, shape into one-inch balls. Wrap in full fat bacon strips and poke each with a skewer. Sauté in the skillet in sizzling hot butter until the sausage meat is cooked and the thin bacon wrapping is crispy. Turn to keep from burning.

Remove from the skillet and deglaze the pan with just a little Offley Ruby port or Asbach cognac. Perhaps a half cup. Scrape all stuck-on bits loose. Strain. You will use this as a dipper sauce.

Position each sausage on a skewer with an Asbach brandy marinated half black mission fig and a firm chunk of your favorite blue cheese. A perfect opportunity to use Stilton. Serve immediately at room temperature.

In the skillet. reduce the deglaze, add a little congealed figgy *jus* or some of your favorite honey or maple syrup. Spritz with white balsamic vinegar. Add a knob of butter. Don't stir. Just swirl the skillet. You should have about a quarter cup of dipping sauce to drizzle over your serving skewers.

This special treat is a grand accompaniment to my spectacular Caesar salad served with crispy black-olive bread croutons. Lay a loaded skewer across the top of each salad plate.

For an alternate way to serve the pigs in a blanket, prepare ice cold butter puff pastry and bake in cut squares. Top each square with a ready to eat piggy. Or, you could wrap each ready-to-eat piggy in a phyllo pastry sac and bake on high heat (400 F) on a cookie sheet, just until the phyllo is crisp.

Serve as individuals or top the Caesar salad with three piggy phyllo sacs.

It's *all* About the Sweet (Medjool) Date.

Medjool dates and my cream cheese pastry (or frozen puffs; even pizza).

Coarsely chop room-temperature Medjool dates (about a pound).

Simmer the dates in a half cup of Asbach Uralt cognac for just a few minutes. Remove from heat, cover and let steep for about 10 minutes. Sprinkle with just a little salt.

Remove the dates with a slotted spoon. Mash with a potato masher. Add a half cup of figgy *jus* from your marinating jar to the cognac pot. Simmer. Reduce by half. The reduction should be a sticky, gooey spread. Add the date mash back to the pot. Stir.

Using my recipe for cream cheese pastry, while still hot, top the flaky baked pastry, cut into two-inch squares and using a spoon of the date mash and top with a piece of room temperature blue cheese. Drizzle a small spoon of my wonderful tomato butter over the blue cheese. Serve right away at room temperature.

Alternate: You can also serve the cognac figgy date mash on a rectangle bed of frozen puff pastry (follow package baking directions). Egg wash the edges of the rectangle. When the pastry puffs, this tasty treat is ready to eat. Drizzle with just a little of your favorite red pepper jelly, warmed in a skillet or even cold from the fridge.

Or, you can prepare mini frozen puff rounds and then fill the warm or room temperature pastries with the date mash. Use a pastry ring to cut.

Another idea: Paste the cognac date mash in a thick layer, add a few candied walnuts and chop a few candied orange rinds from your citrus sugar jar onto my Stollen dough. And continue that recipe, instead of using the Christmas fruit mix.

For a wildly wonderful treat, you can even top homemade pizza with the date mash. Spread the mash on the pizza dough, instead of tomato sauce base, and bake as usual.

Fresh from the oven, drop generous bits of room temperature Brie over the pizza. Lots of Brie. Spritz with a little figgy *jus*. Grind fresh cracked peppercorns and sprinkle on a little salt.

Add crispy fried half-inch pieces of bacon on top. Chop a Bosc pear and sprinkle a few of your favorite nuts on top. Candied walnuts are wonderful. Drizzle with just a little of the bacon fat and cut the pizza in pie-shape wedges.

Make plenty. Your unusual gourmet pizza will be a hit.

Now for the dinner-table special treat:

Medjool dates and maple syrup pork chop cream

Marinate a center cut thick pork chop on the bone, for just a few minutes, in just a little oil, a sprinkle of nutmeg, pepper and a little garlic salt on both sides, and paint both sides with a little Dijon mustard. Sprinkle with salt just when ready to pan fry. Use a rubber scraper to wipe the marinating plate liquid into the skillet.

Melt butter in a hot, stainless-steel skillet. There's already enough oil on the chop that will mix with the hot butter. Set the timer for three minutes. Sear the pork chop, turn down the heat, reset the timer for three minutes and sear the other side. Check doneness. Cooking time will depend on the thickness of the chop.

Tent the skillet with foil, then move the skillet to a turned-off burner and re-check for doneness. The chop should be just cooked. Be careful not to overcook. Remember, the chop will continue to cook in its own heat while resting, tented. Remove from the skillet to a plate to rest, tented.

Deglaze the pan with Asbach Uralt brandy and reduce, scraping the stuck-on pork chop bits.

Slice the chop in thin slices on the diagonal when ready to serve.

Spoon a little puddle of Medjool date maple syrup cream sauce (see instructions below) on a serving plate. Arrange the sliced pork chop off to one side. Dress with fresh leaves of basil, sage and or tarragon and fresh chopped parsley. And if you like, decorate the plate with candied citrus rinds from your pantry citrus sugar jar and a few candied kumquats or mandarin orange slices.

To make the Medjool date maple syrup cream sauce: Every kitchen should have a mini-processor. They cost about $20 in housewares departments in such stores as Canadian Tire. They are worth every penny and don't require much storage space.

Grind six or eight Medjool fresh sweet dates. A big sweet lump will form. Push out the date lump into the still hot butter oil pan juices and deglazing liquid. Mash with a fork, stirring constantly over low heat. Drizzle three tablespoons of maple syrup over the mashed dates. Keep the skillet hot on minimum heat so the dates don't burn. Sprinkle a little salt.

Note: You could substitute three tablespoons of figgy jus from your marinating jar for the maple syrup.

Now you can make this sauce as plain or fancy as you like. It stores well in a covered glass container in the fridge. If preparing a plain sauce, add a cup or more half and half cream and increase heat to incorporate the bubbly hot cream with the mashed dates, stirring constantly. A most beautiful sauce will happen right before your eyes. If it gets too thick, add more cream and incorporate well.

If you want to dress up the sauce, sauté finely chopped onions in butter and add to the sauce. You could add chopped fresh tomatoes, and/or chopped sautéed bell peppers.

As a side, offer a wide flat soup bowl of al dente, your choice of pasta noodles. Fresh homemade pasta is wonderful. Top the pasta with the hot, fresh, Medjool maple syrup cream sauce, grate fresh peppercorns and sprinkle with shards or grated Sartori BellaVitori Raspberry Ale Cheese.

Beyond yum. A most unusual combination of flavors. The result is a sweet savory sauce that can be used on many dishes. (Take into consideration that Medjool dates are very sweet).

A Caesar salad is a nice pairing if you wish to add a salad on a side plate.

Make a bruschetta with toasted slices of black-olive bread, topped with coarsely chopped brandy marinated black mission figs, a little chopped oil packed sun-dried tomatoes and chopped green, red pepper-stuffed Manzanilla olives. Sprinkle with your favorite nuts. Top with grated mozzarella cheese or gobs of Celebrity label Canadian goat cheese (even my marinated goat cheese pucks) and pop under the broiler for just seconds. Drizzle with a little of the Medjool date maple syrup cream sauce.

Flash Un Kas

This fantastic recipe makes about eight dozen bite-size delights. If this sounds like too many, cut the recipe in half. I did that the first time I made them and boy, was I sorry. I hardly got to eat any. They just disappeared. They can be filled with nearly anything that strikes your fancy. I made some with liverwurst and others with lobster paste and creamed crab.

Work together two cups of flour and a half-pound of cream cheese. Chill thoroughly overnight. Take pieces of the dough and roll them very thin, quickly, on a floured board. Preheat the oven when you cut out the dough.

Cut with a round cookie cutter or small glass and fill with the mixture of your choice. Fold in half, close and bake at 400 F for about 10 minutes.

Reheat for serving or make them ahead and bake just before guests arrive. Flash un kas can be frozen.

Alternate: Fresh King crab, claw meat, chopped mashed macerated, marinated in Asbach Uralt brandy, black mission figs, cream cheese, pinch of mustard.

Simple Simon Sandwiches

It's the KISS method—Keep it Simple, Simon.

I've heard people say it's too expensive to shop at the deli counter, buying fresh-cut lunch meats; yet those same people will spend bigger dollars at a drive thru or a food court. To each his own, but fresh is always better, and likely better food.

These are plain and simple sandwiches but there's nothing ordinary about them:

Honey maple ham and Jarlsberg light extra thin Norway cheese, on Dimpflmeier brand 7-grain fresh bread slices:

Butter this soft, wonderful bread right to the edge and use shredded (minced) ham. Ask the deli to cut it fresh for you and double-check that they understand what "mince" means.

I have no idea why this ham tastes better shredded (minced), but it does. All the items here came from a local grocery deli counter, where I stand and watch them shred and slice to special order. Many supermarkets offer fresh deli counter meats and cheeses. Ask for taste tests—they are more than happy to provide them. I don't buy pre-cut at the deli because it gets dry. And I haven't bought pre-packaged sliced meats in probably 50 years. If you were to read the packaging, you wouldn't buy it either. Chock full of preservatives.

My fresh **homemade egg salad** on a plain toasted, buttered English muffin warm, just freshly made or room temperature (not yet refrigerated) is an ideal way to start the day, or pack it and take in a lunch bucket.

Avocado slices with salt and pepper and real bacon and slices of fried potato on toasted whole wheat English muffin is another option. It could be leftover hash browns or latke.

If eating at home, top it with a runny poached egg—and for a spectacular start to your day, top it with fresh-made hollandaise sauce. This sandwich will keep you sated for several hours. ***Alternate to the avocado***: A sliced fresh, firm, juicy peach.

Slice your **favorite steak**, barbecued, broiled, pan-fried, whatever way you like it best, on the diagonal into very thin slices (ask your butcher about tri-tip or skirt steak). Sprinkle with salt and pepper, even if you seasoned it when you cooked it (also great way to use leftover roast beef).

Serve on your favorite grilled crostini bread as an open face sandwich or between two slices of bread as a closed sandwich; as an alternative, load beef slices into a large wonderful pink sun-dried tomato tortilla, once over lightly warmed in a dry sauté pan. Drizzle with my Spectacular barbecue serving sauce, fill and roll and tuck the ends in like a package.

An alternate choice of sauce for your beef sandwiches: Drizzle my favorite, anchovy-free Caesar salad dressing over the beef. Or, spread small dollops of my homemade tomato butter over the cold leftover beef, not on the bread. Or, just drizzle the beef slices with extra virgin olive oil and white wine vinegar, 3:1, mixed with mustard and gooey oven roasted garlic. Put the oil and vinegar in a little empty spice jar with a screw-top lid. Shake and serve. Maybe add a little mesclun green.

Homemade mayo works well with the sliced roast beef sandwiches when you add fresh grated horseradish. For leftover meatloaf or a meatball sandwich, drizzle a squirt of mustard. Try it on fresh generously buttered rye bread. Top with a split dill pickle. For a special treat: Batter and deep-fry thin pickle slices. Amazing!

For leftover chicken: Pick the bones. Add fresh ground pepper. Top with my special homemade Caesar salad dressing or mayo, modified with sour cream added and fresh dill, or fresh grated horseradish, or fresh grated Parmesan. *Very yum!*

For vegetarians: Make a veggie sandwich using shredded sautéed browned Brussels sprouts, top with crunchy bean sprouts and a thick slice of red beefsteak tomato. Drizzle with extra virgin olive oil and white wine vinegar 3:1.

Sandwich alternates: Leftover broccoli rabe or even sautéed cauliflower. Drizzle with white wine vinegar, spritz with extra virgin olive oil, 1:3 and top with crushed candied walnuts from your pantry jar. Add thick slices of avocado, spritzed with fresh squeezed lime juice.

Try this:
On a warm round of focaccia bread with rosemary and other herbs...

Top the focaccia with Norway light Jarlsberg thin cheese slices. Top the cheese with drained cognac marinated black mission figs and little pockets of shredded honey maple ham. Tuck in a few roasted red and yellow peppers. And chopped sun-dried tomatoes.

Split a handful of Manzanilla pepper stuffed olives. Spritz with a spray mix of extra virgin olive oil and white wine vinegar 3:1. Cover with slivers of my caramelized baguette style onions.

Dot with a little more Norway cheese and pop under the pre-heated broiler for just seconds.

Chances are that you haven't had a sandwich like this before.

Croissant Sandwich—Honey Ham and Surprise

Split a fresh soft full-size croissant in half lengthwise. Butter both sides with unsalted butter. (Now's a good time to use your herbed butter log coins.) Any choice: Bell pepper butter, Asbach strawberry butter, herbed butter…mound one side of the croissant with a generous portion of shredded (minced, not sliced) honey ham. On the other side, place three or four overlapping, generous size but thin-sliced provolone cheese slices.

On top of the ham, drizzle a little figgy *jus* from your black mission fig marinating Asbach Uralt cognac jar. I know it sounds like an odd combination, but on top of the cheese slices, cover completely with paper-thin slices of sweet peppery, crunchy, red radishes. The crispiness is grand. If you have homemade candied walnuts and or a candied citrus rind sugar jar, sprinkle a few of either or each on the sandwich, just before you serve.

Put the two halves of the sliced croissant together and indulge in a wonderful tasty sandwich, the likes of which you might not have ever enjoyed before. You might want to cut the sandwich in half, on the diagonal. This is a wonderful lunchbox, carry-it-to-work treat. Wrap and pack separately, with a frozen gel-bag to keep the croissant fresh. No leaking, and the crunch will stay crisp.

You probably won't want mustard or mayonnaise, but if you do, squirt on a bit of my honey mustard sauce, or a smear of my spectacular Caesar salad dressing.

Alternate: You could substitute a few very thin crispy apple slices for the radishes, for another choice. You will see there's no lettuce in this sandwich, but you could always shred any lettuce and add.

And for another day: Substitute thinly shredded leftover roast beef for the honey ham and complete the croissant sandwich as above.

Portobello Sandwiches

Spritz with olive oil and grill portobello mushrooms on high heat on a preheated barbecue.

Make a hungry man dinner sandwich using the large grilled mushrooms instead of bread.

Top one mushroom with roasted chopped mixed color bell peppers, grilled Spanish onions, chopped or sliced. A fat thick slice of beefsteak tomato from your own garden is a great addition, along with a big crispy lettuce leaf.

Chopped garlic or oven roasted garlic, if it is your love, creates a dream combo.

In a stovetop pot, scald a cup of half-and-half cream. Let rise and fall three times. Turn off heat, stirring the cream so it doesn't burn.

Add a half cup of your favorite blue cheese. Stir to incorporate. But leave lumps. Grind a few black peppercorns. Remove the pan from heat. Let it sit briefly. The sauce will thicken and coat a spoon.

Drizzle the warm sauce over the roasted peppers and onions. Position a second portobello mushroom on top or serve as an open-face sandwich. Now you have a delicious spectacular portobello sandwich. It tastes like steak.

To make a larger meal, as a side, serve giant <u>pommes frites</u> or <u>zucchini fries</u>.

A French onion soup, topped with under the broiler yummy Mozzarella cheese and sprinkled with miniature garlic baguette slices on the melted cheese that you have toasted until crunchy, will make for a memorable meal.

Simple Simon says enjoy!

Oh, and don't forget your goat cheese grilled cheese sandwich in my [open and include recipes] <u>REM spinach column</u>. (Scroll down to Comments.)

Stewed Prunes, Oxtails and Oranges

Stewed prunes (plums), bought ready to use in a large glass bottle, can be made into a delightful sauce. Plus, oxtail recipes, dumplings and a word about food storage spaces.

I was rearranging my pantry shelf, and it's a rare thing to find things in tins, but I came across a large container of preserved prunes. And I decided it was time to use them again. This is a quick and easy sauce to make and it keeps well in a glass-covered container in the fridge for several days.

Remove the prunes using a strainer or a slotted spoon and put the liquid into a saucepan. Measure the liquid and add half as much granulated sugar and a cup of Offley Ruby Port.

Bring it to a gentle simmer and reduce by a third. Stir well with a wooden spoon to incorporate the sugar.

Mash the moisture-filled prunes or pulse coarsely. Add a pinch of salt.

Stir the mashed prunes into the reduced sauce pot, on simmer. Squeeze the juice of a fresh sweet orange into the pot and add orange segments from another whole orange, cut from between the membranes.

You could add the zest of a fresh orange or mince a few rinds from your candied citrus sugar jar to finish the sauce, just when ready to serve.

Alternate: You might consider adding a large dollop of sour cream to the port sauce; if you do, do not reheat. The sauce will separate. Just gently fold in the sour cream at the last minute and serve.

Remove the cooked oxtails from their cooking pot (see below), using a spider spoon, and cover with the port prune sauce on a serving platter. Gourmet at its best.

This sauce can also be used over top of pan-fried pork loin medallions (you can substitute veal medallions) or over center-cut grilled thick pork chops. It's a wonderful accompaniment to roasted whole unstuffed Rock Cornish hens that have been roasted with my kumquat marmalade spread over the birds in the last few minutes of roasting. Or, use this prune port sauce with pan-fried duck breast, served medium rare, or over my turkey roll recipe at this link.

Paired with a citrus panna cotta or citrus zabaglione, made with minced rind from your pantry citrus sugar jar, you could even serve dessert in a matching puddle of your main course port prune sauce (save a bit before you add the oxtails). You might top a martini glass of the pudding with a dollop of Port Chantilly Crème (the kind used as filling for my Bird's Nest Pavlova recipe). Or, top an espresso with a tiny spoon of the ruby port cream.

Suggested pairing: Offley Ruby Port. Let it breathe. Serve at a cool room temperature from a narrow neck decanter or directly from its bottle, chilled just a bit.

Another idea: Drizzle the prune port sauce on my grilled goat cheese spinach sandwich recipe you can find here. [open link and include recipe] Scroll down to comments for Grilled Goat Cheese Spinach Sandwich Special (and so much more …)

Or, enjoy the sauce on an open face grilled brown bread slice, topped with thinly sliced roasted turkey and crispy bacon. Very yummy, either way. Note: If you have found a place to buy English bloomer bread that is very popular in U.K., it grills wonderfully. It's also perfect to serve with scrambled eggs and smoked salmon at breakfast.

Asbach Oxtails

In a heavy, coated, cast-iron pot, sauté oxtails in hot butter until brown. Add salt, pepper, Italian seasoning and a sprig of dry, fresh thyme. When cooked, add a little chopped parsley.

Add the following to the pot, then cover: Sweat a large Spanish onion, chopped medium fine; three celery sticks, chopped small but coarse; three carrots, large, cut in pennies on the diagonal.

Add one quart (four cups) of homemade chicken stock and bring to a boil. Turn the heat down. Simmer two hours. During the last half hour of cooking, add a quarter cup of Asbach brandy. Reduce. Sauce will thicken slightly.

You can serve the oxtails dish at this stage. Or, you can remove the oxtails so they don't continue cooking (don't overcook the meat) and add half and half cream. Bring to a boil, turn down the heat (don't cover the pot) and reduce just slightly.

Serve over whipped, mashed potatoes, wide egg noodles or Basmati rice. Also good with crepes. Fill the crepes with the oxtails and serve the crepes in a reduced puddle of the natural sauce or the cream sauce, with the veggies on the plate pushed to the side.

If you have never eaten oxtails, you are missing out on a wonderful dish; but bear in mind, this is exceptionally rich and will be a great surprise for guests, too.

A different approach: Using either method, right at the end, add a tin of whole tomatoes and liquid; break up the tomatoes just a little.

Then, if you would rather have oxtail tomato soup, add another quart of homemade chicken stock. Bring to a boil, turn down heat and serve. When ready to serve, top each individual serving with a few shavings of frozen Asbach butter from your always at-the-ready freezer supply. Do not stir. Just let the compound butter melt.

More Amazing Oxtails: Hungarian Oxtail Goulash

Prepare as above: Let the meat fall off the bones; pull apart the meat using two forks. Reduce the sauce a little on low heat.

Check seasoning. Adjust salt, pepper and add a heaping tablespoon of Hungarian sweet paprika (not the smoky version, unless that is your personal preference). Gently fold in, just before serving, a large scoop of firm full fat sour cream. Do not reheat after adding the sour cream. Keep the cooking pan hot, covered until serving.

Serve the Hungarian oxtail goulash in a large family-style presentation in a large deep platter, along with a bed of my homemade sauerkraut. This works well as a side dish with plain breaded Wiener schnitzel or breaded chicken cutlets or pork cutlets and a generous serving of homemade egg noodles or spaetzle.

A Word About Food Storage Spaces

If you live near a grocery store or market, go in off-hours when checkout lines are less likely to be busy. And go more often. Most people never have enough refrigerator space no matter how big the fridge is, and kitchen cabinet space is often at a premium.

The luxury of having a separate pantry is just that. Unless you have one set, dedicated cabinet for food storage items, it's better to shop frequently. It's never a long walk to the basement and a worthwhile investment to put dedicated shelving in place for things best kept in a cool dark place.

Many Italian-built homes have a cantina. It's not a real cantina unless it has an open air-exchange hole (as a listing rep be careful how you identify that space; you could find yourself paying to modify it). But nonetheless it is a cold room. But be careful about condensation accumulating. Keep an eye open for mold. That is never acceptable.

Back in the pre-war days, and even sometimes after, one could find dedicated giant storage bins in house basements, under a removable basement window, allowing those who grew their own potatoes and root vegetables a means of putting a slide in place and loading wagon-loads of veggies onto slides that delivered the homegrown wonders right to the storage bins, where they provided family food all through the off-seasons. Bins were made from bug-free woods, never from shipping skids that might carry uninvited guests in transit.

Some people who didn't have open-slat wooden basement bins used open hemp sacks for storage. The coal or wood-fired furnace was often in the basement, so that kept any dampness at bay. In Canada, many basement areas had earthen floors.

Although the European immigrants brought their wonderful recipes from overseas with them, some foodstuffs really are international. Made with a local twist. Here is a good example:

Stale Bread Austrian-Style Dumplings

This is another wartime and post-wartime dish. Today we are still in a war—against food pricing and waste.

Bread is bread wherever you go or wherever you live. For these wonderful bread dumplings, you can use almost any bread. It just so happens the dumplings are still a staple in Northern Italy and Austria. And a particular favorite, too, among travelers to the region.

Don't waste those easily dried out baguettes or rolls that become rock hard, almost impossible to bring back to life: French, Italian or Portuguese. Put the dried-out bread in a large plastic bag, lay a clean lightweight tea towel over it, and using your meat pounder hammer, smash the dried bread into large pieces.

Place the bread chunks into a large glass bowl. Just barely cover with half and half cream. The bread will expand as it absorbs the liquid. Let the bread sit for a few hours. You don't want the bread soggy. Just moist.

Regular readers might notice I rarely use milk in my recipes. I don't drink milk and haven't since I was preschool when I was forced to drink milk that was "off". I could never bring myself to drink it again, although very occasionally, I would succumb to a hot chocolate or a milkshake. To me, ever after, milk tastes like whatever the cow had eaten, so I simply avoided it completely. Milk is full of natural sugars. Cream is not. Fat, yes. Sugar, no.

Now for these dumplings some people use flour as a binder. For an exception, perhaps use almonds or hazelnuts that have been ground to a powder flour-like texture. For six cups of soaked moistened bread, use about three-quarters cup of ground nuts (or flour). Whisk a large fresh egg and mix into the moistened bread. Sprinkle with minced fresh parsley and fresh lemon thyme. Grate a little fresh nutmeg into the mix and a little salt and pepper.

Now for the special touch: Add a half cup of my special minced spinach mix from your fridge or thawed overnight freezer storage. But use spinach to which you have added chopped crispy bacon (not store-bought bacon bits).

To see my spinach special recipe scroll down to the sandwich comments here.

The dumplings need to be a generous size, about the size of a cup. Roll scoops of the bread mixture in your dry floured hands to form a ball shape. Dredge in seasoned flour. Cover on a tray with a clean tea towel.

Gently poach the bread dumplings in a large uncovered pot of simmering homemade chicken broth, perhaps for six minutes. Using a spider spoon, gently move the dumplings around in the broth. Do not overcook them.

Pull the dumplings apart into two pieces using two forks and sprinkle with Parmesan and serve alongside my Tiroler mushroom and cheese-filled Wiener schnitzel and spaetzle with a side of my special red cabbage or homemade sauerkraut. The dumplings are also a wonderful side with my sacrilegious Shiraz veal or with my delicious oxtail goulash.

This is a Hungry-Man Meal for sure.

Any leftover dumplings can be sliced about a half-inch thick the next day and reheated quickly in sizzling butter and served with sugared carrots and blanched sweet peas or minty mushy peas.

Alternate: Mince white button mushrooms and minced onion, equal parts. Just sauté once over lightly in sizzling butter, cool slightly and add a little to the moist bread mix. With or without the spinach mix.

Another alternate: Coarsely chop cooked lobster claw meat and mix into the bread dumpling mix. You can keep on hand a flash frozen tin of lobster for this purpose (thaw and squeeze out the liquid; freeze the liquid and save for another recipe) or buy ready-cooked lobster claw packages. Add a little minced fresh tarragon. Poach the dumplings in chicken stock or homemade fish stock.

When ready to serve, spritz with homemade lobster oil or melt a lobster compound butter puck from your stored log and pour over each melt-in-your-mouth seafood dumpling.

Serve the large dumplings as a side, with a tiny drizzle of Petite Maison white truffle Dijon, with a generous bowl of thick Canadian seafood chowder or lobster bisque.

Plums Up! Or Figgy Dumplings

Prepare the bread dumplings using cognac marinated plums or black mission figs, finely chopped (squeeze out excess liquid) and drizzle each dumpling with a little Chantilly Cream and offer a starter as a unique large amuse bouche.

There's nothing difficult about preparing your meals in a gourmet fashion as a home cook. As my readers know, nothing goes to waste in my kitchen. And busy Realtors have to eat, so cooking at home actually saves time because you have an opportunity to multi-task. It's simply a matter of being organized—*mis en place*. Just like at the office.

Make It a Burger Event

When the season is right (any time of year) and the grilling urge strikes, try my selection of gourmet burgers. Some might be a first for my readers. It's easy to multitask since much can be prepared ahead of time.

When the season is right (any time of year) and the grilling urge strikes, try my selection of gourmet burgers. It's easy to multitask since much can be prepared ahead of time.

Prepare your favorite generous burger, but the difference is how you serve it. Your favorite could be ground lamb, pork, veal, chicken, goat or even venison.

Don't overcook the burger. It will continue to cook in its own heat. Choose your favorite bun; maybe try a brioche.

Drizzle the bread with just a little ghee (clarified butter) and grill quickly—only a minute, you don't want the bun to be crunchy.

Place a couple of softened marinated Celebrity brand wonderful creamy Canadian goat cheese pucks from your marinating jar, on each top and bottom grilled bun.

Add a dollop of Wildly Delicious Beet and Red Onion Marmalade or my tomato butter on each half on top of the cheese. Or if you want something really different, use my kumquat marmalade.

Top the marmalade with a teaspoon of Petite Maison White Truffle Dijon. Spritz with Black Maple Magic Balsamic Vinegar, add a generous amount of fresh watercress, and position your burger between the two bun pieces.

Make plenty. There won't be leftovers.

You could add crumbled crispy bacon just before you serve. (Not store-bought bacon bits.)

A good pairing: Stella Belgian beer, or Molson Export Ale. Both act as a purposeful palate cleanser between delicious bites. Overseas, people prefer to drink their beer at room temperature, but this side of the ocean it's preferred cold. Never put ice in beer, but it is said real beer drinkers add a pinch of salt to the empty cold glass before pouring.

Norwegian Steelhead Burger

Grill both halves of a brioche bun. Spritz with extra light virgin olive oil. Smear each side with my warm blue cheese dressing. Place a beautiful large hydroponic Boston Bibb lettuce leaf on each half. Add a tablespoon of my shredded green apple (unpeeled) fennel slaw to each half. Then add a generous mound of paper-thin Norwegian frozen/thawed steelhead smoked salmon napkins. (This product sounds expensive and it is, but it feeds dozens of people, dozens of times. It thaws very quickly so it is handy always to have on hand, so you can gourmet many things in just minutes. Well-wrapped, double-wrapped in plastic wrap, it keeps for ages in the freezer. I cut the very long package in half to position easier in the freezer, and only take out half at a time to work with.)

On top of the Norwegian salmon mound, add a few very thin slices of Norwegian light Jarlsberg cheese. This wonderful cheese is almost sweet. It has holes in it like we typically see in Swiss Cheese. This cheese is nothing short of excellent. Ask the deli to slice it very thin, if not already prepared that way. Next, slice paper-thin raw red onion and add a generous amount to finish this wonderful treat. The smoked salmon loves red onion.

This is likely a burger like you've never had before. There's a good chance you will make it often.

Serve with a cheese board of mixed cheeses you might not normally indulge in, giving guests an opportunity to try something unusual like Celebrity brand Sartori raspberry delicious shards, and perhaps their Espresso cheese.

Pairs wonderfully with unoaked shiraz or with my old standby, Winzertanz.

A Fish Burger? Maybe A Fishwich

It's another fishy thing! Build a burger using a mound of freshly made breaded fish nuggets topped with my amazing Caesar salad dressing. Yes. You read it right. (Now, if you really want a spectacular "seawich," go completely overboard and use once over-lightly, butter-seared scallops—not the tiny bay scallops, for a spectacular treat.)

Position a juicy split brandy marinated black mission fig on top of the dressing. And add shredded romaine lettuce and sprinkle with fresh grated Parmesan. Amazing! Want to get a little over the top? Use pre-cooked lobster claw meat as an alternate to the nuggets…Or my lobster tails.

A side dish of my special Waldorf Salad rounds out the meal.

Super Crabby Burger

Grill both halves of buttered brioche. Prepare crab meat, leaving large chunks visible, adding finely chopped celery, a tiny pinch of minced onion, salt, pepper, sweet paprika and a little white truffle Dijon, stirred into mashed cream cheese. Fold in a tablespoon of full fat sour cream.

Mound the crab meat mixture on loads of crispy ordinary iceberg lettuce leaves (or shredded) on the grilled, buttered, brioche bun.

If you enjoy heat, drizzle a little of your favorite hot sauce onto the crab mix. Sprinkle with sweet paprika and/or cayenne. Drizzle with my warm blue cheese dressing, to which you have added a pinch of mashed homemade roasted garlic. If you enjoy horseradish, a tiny bit of homemade horseradish cream is a nice completer, or add a dollop of my Hazelnut Pesto for a different experience. Crispy arugula added at the last minute makes this a delightful burger.

My Remoulade Sauce for Shrimp Po'boy Burger

In a blender, start with three whole eggs. Add two coarsely chopped white garlic cloves, a tablespoon of white truffle Dijon, zest of a half lemon and fresh squeezed half lemon juice.

Add a teaspoon of freshly grated raw horseradish. Add a generous raw shallot, split in four, and a half teaspoon of raw onion. Two large fresh basil leaves zip up the flavors.

Add a teaspoon of sweet paprika and a sprinkle of cayenne, salt, "garlic scape sea salt" and a teaspoon of ground chili powder. Add very high-quality fresh ground pepper and a half teaspoon of Sambul (the East Indian islands spice) and whir the blender to combine.

From your pantry citrus jar, chop a quarter cup of mixed candied citrus rind. Add to blender ingredients. Cover and pulse to mince. Add a quarter cup of the best-quality thick maple syrup. Drizzle in Mazola Corn Oil just gradually while machine is running, until the consistency is that of thick mayonnaise.

Serve as a dipping sauce for butterflied batter-fried shrimp that you have filled a grilled split ghee-spritzed baguette with.

You can drizzle my remoulade onto the po'boy burger, but only just when you are ready to eat, so you don't make the breaded shrimp soggy.

No words to say how good this hot sauce is. You could use it with any of the burgers if you like a memorable hot Cajun mouth-watering experience. (Not for serving to children.)

Tomato Peach Fruit Carpaccio

Check out the colors.

For this recipe, you should prepare all the items ahead of time but keep everything separate and refrigerated. Assemble it near to serving time. Choose very firm fresh tomatoes so they don't leak their water content onto the plate.

When preparing to serve, select a large rectangular serving platter, smear the plate with either my special Caesar salad dressing or use my warm, fresh amazing blue cheese dressing; if you love garlic, when using either sauce, stir in a little oven-roasted light golden color garlic purée from your refrigerated jar, as much or as little as you like; then arrange the fruit in symmetrical rows, overlapped with quite thick slices of fresh firm juicy tomatoes with equal thickness slices of fresh firm, skinned peaches.

An even more interesting plate: use yellow tomatoes with the yellow peaches or go completely different and use white tomatoes and white peaches. Yes, they both are available white.

Depending on where you live you might have to ask your green grocery department to order in for you. So, get organized well ahead of time so you know where you can buy what when you are ready.

Both fruits love fresh ground pepper, so use plenty, and just a little granular salt. If you can find it in a specialty shop, use garlic scape sea salt.

Just before serving, use room temperature sauce again to drizzle overtop the fruits. Yes, tomato is a fruit.

Serve this platter buffet-style along with a cognac marinated black mission fig tarte tartin, and a pie-shaped piece of warm, baked, smoked Norwegian salmon frittata, made with minced dill, a little mustard and Canadian goat cheese, using a dozen whisked eggs, a little flour, baking powder, salt, pepper and a bit of oven-roasted garlic purée.

Bake the frittata in a stainless-steel sauté pan with an oven-proof handle, on the center rack on high heat, perhaps at preheated 400 F to 450 F.

Know your oven. If baking in glass, always drop the oven temperature 25 degrees. Test at a half hour but allow 45 minutes just in case. Set your timer.

The frittata is done when a knife inserted comes out clean. It's no different than a baked custard. It will keep overnight in the fridge but remove it in plenty of time to serve at room temperature, or then reheat for a few minutes only at 200 F. Pre-cut into individual servings but serve in the baking dish with a pie piece serving lifter.

And the table pièce de resistance…add a whole beautiful round genoise, filled with fresh fruit and stiff Chantilly cream, to the table.

Remove one serving size wedge, so people can see what's inside, and provide a long, thin serrated knife and a pie slice lifter so people can decide for themselves whether they prefer a tiny piece or an extra-large serving.

An urn of fresh brewed hot coffee might be appreciated, or even espresso (hint: make the genoise filling coffee cream).

Depending on what fruit you choose in the genoise filling, provide a matching fruit coulee in a small gravy boat, with a little ladle, in case someone might like a fresh fruit drizzle on their cream-covered genoise.

You could substitute a fruit cream-filled homemade, layered, horizontally sliced pound cake, completely covered in Chantilly cream and decorated using a forcing bag with a large star tip.

Use an offset spatula to spread the Chantilly and a sharp knife to slice, or you could pre-slice and overlap the slices on a generous rectangular serving platter. Surround with whole fruits; perhaps a mix of whole strawberries, raspberries, blueberries, blackberries or even gooseberries.

It's a royal exquisite buffet table selection that is light and beautiful to look at as eye candy, making it even more delectable on the palate.

Easy to prepare; takes no time at all, and it's all so fresh. The genoise can be made a day ahead, sliced into three horizontal slices, ready to fill just before preparing the buffet table, but refrigerate either finished cream cake until the last minute.

Invest in a large plastic dome container to cover whipped cream cakes, to avoid their taking on any fridge fragrances. For example, if you have sliced fresh cucumbers in the fridge, remove them if you are storing whipped cream covered cakes.

Always add fresh cut flowers or at the very least, a generous flowering potted plant placed strategically or use a row or grouping of little pots artfully arranged in pretty little soup cups perhaps. If it happens to be pansy season or nasturtium time, they make great little container fillers as table pretty helpers, mixed with little bunches of fresh herbs for a little greenery.

Maybe choose a loud contrasting color mix, or pair up using a matching flower color for synchronizing. For example, if you are doing a white carpaccio, perhaps use stalks of white phlox or wild lupins. Strategically arrange bunches of fresh herbs if no flowers are available.

You could even chop fresh basil or rosemary and scatter all over the table between the food serving plates. Kind of like herb snowflakes. The fragrance is grand. Best perfume in the world, and a natural air-freshener too.

Offer a bowl of lemon wedges for those who would enjoy. Especially nice squeezed over the frittata.

A cheese board and frozen-grape presentation is always welcome. Freeze a cluster of seedless sweet sugar-coated grapes, green or purple. Keep refrigerated until serving time. Bunches of fresh basil are nice on the serving plate, put in place at the last minute.

Extra special treat: For fresh, firm tomatoes, any color: If you have never done this, using a box grater on the course side, push the whole tomato, starting at the bottom tomato end, along the wide grating holes side, until there is only the tomato skin in your hand.

Stand the manual grater on a large plate and all the tomato pulp solids will be on the plate along with a little tomato water. Drain off the liquid (I use a small sieve) and you have the most fabulous tomato pulp that seems to exacerbate the incredible fresh tomato taste.

The fresh pulp can be used for a multitude of things, including a topper for a wonderful omelet, or as a side dish with my fabulous grilled goat cheese sandwich. Or just serve plain and simple as a side dish with any meal. Or mound the pulp on a grilled garlic-smeared bread, sliced on the diagonal to make an amazing bruschetta for a mega special treat.

Chop a little flat leaf parsley or fresh basil and enjoy. You could add herbs and spices, but just plain pulp is amazing. Maybe sprinkle with fresh real parmesan.

Why this process enhances the fruit flavor I have no idea. But it certainly heightens the taste bud experience way over the top. Try it. You might be surprised.

And now for a couple of hints you can't resist. Buy a bottle of sweeter label Prosecco. Ruffino works. Pop the cork as you would champagne. Add it to a mix of peach coulee, made using your food processor and fresh tomato pulp (prepared as above using the box grater) combined with sugar-water syrup to which you have added a little orange juice. Pop the mix into a glass or metal tray that can be frozen.

Just before the mixture is frozen solid, scape from end to end using a fork. Re-freeze and process in this manner three times. Freeze and scrape.

You have made a wonderful "granita," sort of a cross between sorbet and semi-freddo. A wonderful summertime treat that is excellent all year round.

Use an ice cream scoop and serve in a martini glass with a sprig of fresh mint. Works beautifully between courses of a heavy meal, as a palate cleanser. (Perhaps with a venison meal, or stronger game dishes, or roasted rabbit.)

Here's a magical tip for not wasting any leftover Prosecco, for people like me who would have leftovers because I mostly use spirits for cooking. Freeze it in ice cube trays and add it to special sauces, gravies or even to soups; or pop a Prosecco ice cube into a glass of your favorite smoothie or fruit juice or into a fruit coulee, served in a bowl stem wine glass. This ice cube process will prevent the Prosecco from turning to a vinegar taste.

You can make ice cubes from any leftover wines. I know: Some of you will say there are never leftover spirits at your house! Whatever suits your fancy. Many people who live alone avoid buying spirits due to the cost and fear of waste, so this great idea solves that issue.

A Figgy Cornish Hen Christmas

Here's a little different Christmas Eve or Christmas Day special feast. It seems like a lot of work and it's time-consuming but not difficult. And so worth it.

As many of our readers know, I keep a large jar of fresh, not dried, black (blue) mission figs, either Spanish or Italian, in my refrigerator at all times soaking in brandy. (I did try but have not had good luck with the figs from Mexico, so I would not recommend using them.)

If you follow my style, you will have marinated juicy figs and macerated ones that have been longer in the jar. Long ago I discovered that marinating in Asbach Uralt cognac produces a wonderful congealed just as the figs and cognac marry.

So here is a wonderful stuffing, baked in a separate dish and spooned into the hen cavity after the hens are roasted. I know. That sounds a little odd, but the result is wonderful.

You can prepare the stuffing ahead of time. (You can even freeze larger quantities, packaged in full cups so you can choose how much you need; thaw overnight in the fridge the day before using.)

In the oven on a sheet pan, toast a pulled apart loaf of stale bread, or chop into large chunks a loaf of black-olive bread or a couple of baguettes that you have left on the counter overnight to dry. Ideally, you will fill six cups with bread or double the recipe if you are roasting many hens. If there is any leftover stuffing, refrigerate it covered and serve it the next day, perhaps just a breakfast plate (or served hot in an oval au gratin dish) of stuffing with a couple of poached eggs and hollandaise.

Finely chop a couple of split, long celery stalks and mince a few leaves. Add a cup of coarsely chopped Spanish onion and a half teaspoon of your refrigerated homemade oven-roasted golden garlic purée.

Sauté the mix in sizzling butter just briefly. You don't want the celery and onions mushy, but to retain a little crunch. Sprinkle with salt, pepper and a little thyme, a tiny bit of nutmeg and just a pinch of sage.

Let cool. Fold in a generous cup of chopped cognac marinated black mission figs, coarse or fine (but not the macerated ones) and a half cup of the congealed cognac figgy *jus*. Add a cup of coarsely crushed shelled beautiful, green, pistachios. Mix the toasted bread into the sauté pan.

Lightly butter a glass loaf baking dish. Gently pack the stuffing into the dish. Bake in a 325 F (350 F if using a metal dish) preheated oven for about 45 minutes, covered in foil, shiny side in. Remove foil and continue to bake for about another 10 minutes. Let rest on the counter for a half hour. Then spoon the stuffing into the still very hot roasted hen cavities just before serving.

In the last 10 minutes of roasting, the Rock Cornish hens, baste with my kumquat marmalade. Or use a high-quality bitter orange store-bought marmalade. Add a tablespoon of the cognac figgy jus to the marmalade to make it easier to paint on the hens.

I've noted previously that I prefer to roast the hens standing up, and yes they are touching one another, in a preheated oven 400 F; after 15 minutes reduce heat to 350 F. Paint the hot hens with butter at this point, and continue to roast for another half hour, or until juices run clear. Puncture the leg crease to check doneness. Timing will depend on the size of the hens. Make sure to choose ones of nearly equal size. I buy frozen hens and keep a stock in the freezer. Remove the packaging. Thaw in the refrigerator 24 to 48 hours before roasting.

It's important to choose a right size roasting pan, dependent upon the number of hens you are serving. I've done as many as 26 standing medium-size hens, using a large turkey roasting pan or double tinfoil pan, nearly the size of the oven. The kind I would roast a 20 to 23-pound turkey in each Christmas. Allow one whole hen per serving. They are roasted uncovered but cover in foil shiny side in for the first 15 minutes on high heat.

As a special treat, prepare Yorkshire puddings (one or two for each serving) oven roasted in very hot sizzling butter, deflate and fill the hole first with a little well-drained, hot, fresh regular wilted spinach, buttered and topped with just a little extra pistachio stuffing. Deglaze the roasting pan with just a little brandy. You could light it to burn off the alcohol, or if you are experienced, you could just tilt the pan.

Drizzle a little pan dripping deglaze, perhaps a teaspoon (there won't be much drippings) over top of each filled Yorkshire pudding, and just a spritz of extra figgy jus.

Alternate: You could substitute prunes soaked in cognac overnight. Or just choose to use chopped Medjool dates. They are very naturally sweet.

A perfect side dish is buttered, sugared fresh carrots, oven-roasted halved acorn squash, with butter and maple syrup, and/or pan-roasted Brussels sprouts. A creamed Belgian endive is also a great side; any of the above with my special whipped mashed potatoes.

You could offer a serving dish of cranberry sauce, just to be festive. Want something a little different? Chop a macerated black mission fig and add it and a little figgy jus to the cranberry sauce and add a few homemade candied walnuts from your pantry jar.

I like to serve the hens in a place setting of their own in a just right size hot, au gratin oval ovenproof dish, placed on an oversize plate with space where people can serve themselves however many sides they want to add, family style from covered vegetable bowls or hot water heated chafing dishes.

In the kitchen, heat the oversized dinner plates and position the stuffed hens. Deliver the plated hens to the table and place each hot plate onto a large charger on a tablecloth or placemat, to keep a distance between your table and the hot dinner plates.

It's perhaps a little different Christmas Eve or Christmas Day special feast. It seems like a lot of work. It's time-consuming but not difficult. And so worth it.

Just a note: If you feel a must-have need for a salad, my Caesar salad is a nice balance of flavors. And further, if a dessert is absolutely necessary, make it a light cranberry or fig panna cotta that could be made a day before and dressed at the table, or a figgy zabaglione in a martini glass topped with a brandy marinated fig and a drizzle of the cognac figgy jus, or just offer a slice of my Asbach Stollen that you made months before. You could even go overboard and drizzle each slice with your favorite plum pudding sauce.

A centerpiece or multiples made of snipped single flowers from a poinsettia plant add a little festive color to the table. Careful with having live rosemary trees in the house, although they are sold in the festive season. The fragrance can be wonderful or can be overpowering, as are hyacinths brought indoors. Consider that some people have allergies. It's generally safe to use potted herb plants; maybe cover the pot in shiny foil gift wrap and add a candy cane or two.

Holiday Turkey Balls (All Year 'Round)

Just because…Because it's Christmas. Perhaps print this recipe add-on column and roll the paper and tie with a red and or green curled ribbon and pack with a gift to give to a friend or client newsletter list. Holiday ***"Turkey Balls" instead of oven-roasted whole turkey, perhaps.***

In the spirit of the season, a different kind of turkey-bird for the holidays, or for any time, this is a perfect way to enjoy the flavor of the seasonal bird in a little different, very easy to prepare way.

With many families experiencing loved ones not able to get home for the holidays, or sometimes teens away at school, and no longer any need for roasting a big turkey at home, this recipe provides the turkey "taste of the season" in a miniature fashion for those dining alone or with a mate or for just enjoying with a couple of friends. You could even make this and send it off to college kids.

Maybe make some version of this and deliver to a shut-in during the holidays, or to someone in a nursing home or even in hospital if allowed, or perhaps deliver to a new immigrant family living nearby who might never have eaten turkey-bird, to enjoy in the privacy of their own surroundings, whether or not they celebrate our holidays yet. Perhaps pack up in a large seasonal garland bag, a few toss-away dollar-store serving pieces or economical glass pieces, utensils, napkins, and a few festive seasonal table toppers. It's not an expensive addition, and will make a long-lasting impression.

Alternate: Replace the veal and pork with fresh, never frozen, ground turkey, white, dark, or a mixture of each. Ask your meat and poultry counter to grind the turkey fresh, and take a look at what exactly he's grinding, ideally under your watch.

Mince frozen or fresh, barely cooked cranberries that you've sautéed in just enough sizzling butter to coat the pan, and maybe add a drizzle of maple syrup or medium sugar syrup, and add the chopped sautéed cranberries to the other ingredients. You might choose to finely chop a couple of cognac marinated black mission figs and add to the cranberries and a tiny bit of congealed figgy brandy jus instead.

Stir in a quarter cup of homemade chopped candied walnuts from your pantry jar, and maybe even mince a bit of candied citrus rind from your pantry citrus sugar jar.

OR: Just add a little finely chopped brandy marinated black mission figs directly to the ground turkey mix.

When ready to serve, perhaps drizzle with my figgy cream sauce.

Although a terrific *hors d'oeuvres*, these deep-fried (I prefer Mazola Corn Oil for all my deep-frying) breaded turkey balls are also wonderful as an entree, accompanied by my special whipped, mashed potatoes, butter-browned Brussels sprouts with homemade crispy full-fat regular old-fashioned bacon pieces (the reduced-fat, reduced-salt bacon has a distinct chemical taste I find, so after trying various brands, I went back to the original), and sugar-buttered carrots. Or even with halved, baked, acorn squash, served in the green half shell, drizzled with butter and a bit of maple syrup just during last ten minutes of roasting, or add a sprinkle of brown sugar. Squash loves lots of fresh ground pepper and just a little salt.

Or if you are feeling a little nostalgic, perhaps gently pack the ground turkey mix, whichever one you choose to make, into a loaf pan. Cover with foil (always shiny side in 'cause the shiny side deflects the heat) until last ten minutes of roasting. Top with a smear of Dijon during the last ten minutes, in a preheated 350 F oven, placed on center rack.

Remember to drop your oven temperature 25 degrees if you are using a glass baking loaf pan. Roasting likely will take about 45 minutes on middle oven rack. Tent and rest for 10 minutes when finished. Of course, the mix is not breaded on its exterior, so you might choose to treat the turkey loaf mix, instead, as individuals, roasted in a large size muffin tin tray.

An aside:

Just an interesting comment from Michelle Obama: Barack asked for Dijon mustard when he was eating in a very ordinary restaurant on tour pre his election to the US Presidency, while they were travelling cross-country. The people thought his "gourmet" request for Dijon mustard made him appear as thinking he was someone special when he thought no such thing. My, oh my! What a life! And later, in her book, the former First Lady made note that in the White House, the presidential family pays for its own food; they are presented with itemized grocery store bills the staff has accumulated when doing the actual food shopping, including being required to pay for toilet paper. What's to say other than: "Amazing!" This is how people are treated who dedicate their personal lives to the world of politics.

Of course often we take Dijon mustard for granted, and many of us ordinary people use it regularly. Different strokes for different folks. Back when I first started writing my weekly "Gourmet Cooking with Carolyne" newspaper columns, and teaching for the board of education as well as private classes, back in the mid-1970s, so many things we have available in ordinary grocery stores now, were certainly not available back then. I am not a chef, but rather a food writer and original recipe developer, and taught what I learned on an asked for basis. Requests came as a result of the newspaper columns. I still get requests asking if I have created yet my very own certain recipes (just had a request from a young woman who recently had moved here from Brazil. She had learned to cook her local foods under the watchful eye of her grandmother, but was curious about learning new ways to cook, here in her new country).

Now most large-scale grocery stores have special aisles dedicated to imported foods from all over the world, making items like Dijon mustard always available. We now truly live in a multicultural society, reflected in food items in particular, and many specialty stores make the lesser volume items available as specialty items, but not difficult to find. And, of course, for those who shop on line, many unusual items are available with next day delivery.

My personal beef: Buying fresh herbs is an ongoing problem. Certain items, even so grown in greenhouse environments are not always readily available. Fresh, potted, tarragon being a particular point of reference frustration (and seafood loves tarragon). Stores only stock what people en masse, buy, largely due to lack of shelf space that is in high demand for other items.

Herbs don't keep well, although if you wrap them in moist white paper towel and keep in the crisper, they do stay fresh for a few days. But when they dry, simply store them in a glass-covered labeled jar. My bucket list dream is to have one of the new type herb-growing refrigerators that look a little like a small wine fridge. Built initially on a larger scale for restaurant use, and now available in home-size. But being a new and specialty product, they are still price-prohibitive for the average homeowner.

***

Any leftover turkey loaf, sliced, makes a wonderful sandwich on your favorite bread, grilled. Particularly good on my homemade, buttered, grilled, dill bread. You could even top a crostini open face sandwich with a slice, maybe on a bed of my Caramelized onions. Smear the turkey loaf slice with my special tomato butter or offer my "Spectacular Barbecue Serving Sauce" recipe (so much better than ketchup; one reader made it and said she'd never buy ketchup again). And to think I first made it so as not to toss away a leftover half tomato.

A really fun way to serve the deep-fried breaded turkey balls is to stuff a freshly baked Yorkshire pudding, roasted in sizzling butter using a frozen coin from one of my compound butters logs in each hot muffin pan pocket (heat the pan in the oven first, and follow my Yorkshire Pudding recipe); let the puff relax and deflate, then position the turkey ball, whichever way you chose to prepare it. (If you choose to fill a Yorkshire Pudding using a shellfish breaded deep-fried ball, use a sizzling seafood compound butter to oven-roast the Yorkshire Puddings for a completely different presentation.)

You could even serve three regular size breaded deep-fried turkey balls (or shellfish balls) on a skewer with a roasted Brussels Sprout in-between and or a couple of large cranberries, for just a little different serving idea. A great walk-about *hors d'oeuvres*.

And drizzle using any of my wonderful sauces. Enjoy!

AND: "Here's another *Turkey Ball* serving idea…"

Make the balls about a small one-cup size. Of course, they will take longer to cook, breaded, deep-fried in the hot oil (or you could use three smaller ones instead).

Put the turkey ball(s) into a martini glass. Using a large open-star tip nozzle in a piping bag (or snip off a small corner of a plastic sandwich bag), pipe my special whipped, mashed potatoes around the edge of the top of the martini glass, a double round, letting the turkey ball(s) peek through. Drizzle with just a little hot clarified butter. Sprinkle the whipped, mashed potatoes with sweet paprika to add a little color, or dot with a few whole cranberries, interspersed with pimento-stuffed Manzanilla olives. If you have a little herb rosemary tree for the season, pluck off a little branch and position at an angle in the martini glass, or just lay the rosemary twig on the napkin at the edge of the martini glass base. You could place the turkey ball on a small bed (perhaps a teaspoon) of my black mission fig stuffing (baked separately; see separate recipe).

Maybe place a skewer across the top of the martini glass, with three pimento-stuffed Manzanilla olives and a whole cranberry between each. If you made the figgy turkey balls, insert a piece of marinated black mission fig in-between.

A mouth-watering presentation that's pretty and so easily assembled, and everything can be made ahead of time, earlier in the day and reheated in the oven just before assembling in each martini glass.

Place each stemmed martini glass on an *hors d'oeuvres* napkin on a see-through glass plate, on a round placemat, and if you have available, serve with a seafood fork or a salad fork, sitting crosswise alongside the glass stem, along with a soup spoon so you don't miss a drop of this dish that will appeal to everyone.

A side serving of my Caesar Salad is a nice accompaniment.

Note: If you are using this serving idea as part of a large multiple entree special dinner, on some occasion you might like to substitute instead, my breaded deep-fried shellfish seafood balls recipe, and make this martini glass presentation into a wonderful *hors d'oeuvres* course, serving as the turkey entrée course maybe my turkey roll.:
https://www.remonline.com/gourmet-cooking-for-real-estate-professionals-turkey-time/

Bitterballen (veal croquettes).

Traditionally served at New Year's or Christmas, these delightful "meatballs" will have all your guests coming back for seconds and thirds. They are good year-round, not just for special occasions.

The bitterballen are deep-fried and served piping hot with hot mustard; keep them warm in the oven until serving time or make them ahead and reheat in 300 F oven for about half an hour prior to serving. The name is misleading, because there is nothing bitter about them. The name comes from the occasions on which they are served, when "bitters" are frequently offered along with drinks, particularly gin. This is traditionally a Dutch treat, but the following is my own creation and we serve it all year round to family and friends who drop in.

Bitterballen freeze well, so you can always have some on hand. They will keep for several days in the coldest part of the fridge, although they will not keep indefinitely because of the cream content. So, you really don't think much of veal? Kind of blah and tasteless, you say? Your husband wouldn't eat veal, so no sense even trying this recipe? Well, if you insist. Funny, I'm sure he'd be back for seconds at my house.

1 pound ground veal
¼ pound ground pork
Salt, pepper, Italian seasoning
Garlic salt
Thyme

Sage

1 egg; beaten

¾ cup course breadcrumbs, brown or cracked wheat

Chopped parsley

2 tablespoon cream

Seasoned breadcrumbs

Beaten eggs

Oil or lard for deep-frying

Mix all ingredients in large mixing bowl and form 1-inch balls (rather large). Cover with oiled waxed paper if you aren't going to deep-fry them straight away. Roll balls in beaten egg and then in seasoned breadcrumbs. Deep-fry. Test oil with cube of dry bread. Bread should deep-fry to a beautiful golden color on both sides in about 60 seconds; or with thermometer, oil should reach 375 F, not hotter or it will smoke. I always deep-fry using corn oil.

You should always use a deep cast-iron pot or a heavy baked-enamel pot for deep-frying, if you don't have a deep-fryer. Never try to deep-fry in an aluminum pot and do not have liquid fat deeper than half way up the side of the pot. Bitterballen will cook in about 3–4 minutes on each side. Makes about 30. (Plan on 4–6 per person because they'll be back for seconds.)

Shrimp in Garlic Cognac Cream

(And seared sea scallops in duxelles and pink champagne sabayon)

Seared sea scallops in duxelles and pink champagne sabayon

First prepare my duxelles recipe.

Then prepare sabayon, your favorite way. I prefer to use a bain-marie. Preheat the broiler. Place the oven rack in second top position.

In sizzling butter in a stainless-steel sauté pan, perfectly sear three scallops per person. Turn only once. Sprinkle with just a pinch of thyme. The scallop edges should turn a very fine, beautiful, golden color. They take just minutes to cook. Absolutely do not overcook.

Deglaze the pan with a little pink champagne. (I use pink sparkling French Royal de Neuville.) Add the sizzling butter pan juices to the ready sabayon.

Assemble: Using large coquilles, place the shells on a bed of coarse sea salt to stabilize (coarse pickling salt will do since the salt won't come in contact with the food) on a large rimmed baking sheet.

Carefully spoon a little prepared duxelles into each shell. Spritz with a little pink champagne and a pinch of salt and pepper. (Use ground pink peppercorns if available.)

Add a few tablespoons of pink champagne sabayon. Position three seared sea scallops in each shell.

Place the salt sheet holding the coquilles under the preheated broiler oven just for a few minutes and serve immediately.

Alternate: Substitute cognac Asbach Uralt for the champagne for a different but most amazing taste.

For an equally delightful offering, you could change up the whole presentation and instead use another of my "shell-a-brate" recipes, served on a large coquille, also placed under the piping hot broiler for just seconds.

My Ultimate Shrimp in Garlic Cognac Cream

In sizzling unsalted butter, sauté slivered paper-thin garlic slices; about a half cup. That's a sizeable amount of garlic, but you read it right.

Turn the heat down because you want to keep the garlic white. Sauté until the texture is nearly mashable. Sprinkle with a pinch (just a pinch, not more) of ground cloves, a pinch of nutmeg, a pinch of paprika, a little bit of thyme and a little salt and pepper.

Add a little more butter and the shrimp that are still in their shells. 27–30 size. Or as many as you like.

Be careful that the sauté pan is still very hot but not browning. The shrimp will cook in just a couple of minutes; turn only once immediately when the first side turns pink. Shrimp is fully cooked when opaque. Absolutely do not ever overcook. The shrimp will get rubbery.

Remove the pan contents and deglaze the sauté pan with a generous splash of Asbach Uralt cognac. The bouquet will erupt and fill your kitchen with the most amazing perfume.

Now add to the very hot pan, a cup of half-and-half cream (or more if you have doubled the shrimp quantity). Let the cream scald and reduce. The thickened cream will take on the wonderful color of the cognac as well as the fragrance.

Put the shrimp back into the sauté pan and tumble to coat in the amazing sauce.

Using a rubber spatula, wipe the sauce and the lightly coated shrimp completely from the pan into a just right-size serving bowl.

You can serve immediately or at room temperature or even cold the next day. The sauce will congeal overnight as it continues to thicken.

An unspeakable treat. I often refer to this as my "house-selling shrimp dish." I sometimes surprised a neighbor with a pretty glass covered bowl of this quick and easily made recipe. Add a few slices of homemade grilled garlic bread. Great nibbles after work while they barbecue their steaks.

Agents will remind sellers not to offend sensitive noses of maybe-buyers by cooking, especially cabbage or fish, when their house is on the market. When I was selling, I did not take my own advice, as I have mentioned in some posted REM comments over the years. I opened my windows while having appointments and let the mouth-watering vapors waft through the area.

After only a couple of appointments, an offer appeared, along with comments like a reader recently so kindly made: "What time is dinner tonight?"

Total time in the kitchen less than a half hour. And you can't buy or order in this kind of goodness. Really! Try it for yourself. Serve alone or with plain instant one-minute basmati buttered rice. You'll make the neighbors' mouth water. Or serve the shrimp alongside your steak as a very special surf and turf. Surprise yourself!

A tall cool glass of Winzertanz pairs wonderfully. Enjoy!

If you have leftover sauce, don't toss it. Refrigerated, the sauce will keep for a couple of days, covered in a glass container. Use it to tumble over cooked pasta or rice, with added seared fresh sea scallops. Mouth-watering good leftovers.

Or put a small puddle of the leftover sauce on an oversized dinner plate and position fresh deep-fried homemade crab cakes strategically. Drizzle just a little sauce over each crab cake. Top with shards of fresh Parmesan cheese, using your vegetable peeler or kase scharfe.

Decorate the plate with a sprig of fresh basil leaves. Dress with lemon quarters to be squeezed when desired.

Alternate: If you love crushed or flaked fresh coconut, lightly brown it in a single layer, in just a tiny bit of sizzling unsalted butter (in a nearly dry very hot sauté pan). Sprinkle the crispy coconut over the cognac creamed shrimp just when ready to serve. Do not stir.

Another alternate: prepare your favorite salmon steak and during the last minute of sautéing or roasting or grilling, add a little of the leftover cognac sauce. (You could use on any fish.)

As I've said countless times…nothing goes to waste in my kitchen.

Note: A reader used leftover shrimp sauce on an oven-roasted Atlantic salmon steak, just in the last seconds in the oven. Really delicious!

At the table:

With either recipe, offer a tuile or two. Prepare a Parmesan tuile or perhaps a ground almond tuile. There are loads of recipes for these simple, tasty creations.

Prepare the table placing a large, folded, heavyweight cotton tea towel in the center where you can place a large (hot water) heated serving platter or two upon which to place the broiler hot coquilles. In the kitchen, arrange the coquilles on a bed of coarse salt on the large hot platter for presentation as a table center place.

Prepare each place setting with a large charger plate on a cloth covered tabletop or on a placemat, topped with a plain oversized serving plate with a folded-square cloth napkin on each, ready to receive a very hot coquille. Place a seafood fork or pie fork at each place setting, along with a soup spoon to enjoy the sauce and drippings. Place a tuile or two at the edge of each plate.

Pink Champagne Royal Cocktail—My Very Own

Here's a nice pairing to serve: My very own martini creation, using either matching Royal de Neuville or Asbach Uralt cognac, depending on which you used in your recipe choice.

In a cold metal cocktail shaker, pour in a half cup of Asbach Uralt cognac.

Add a half cup of cold sugar syrup made using 50:50 sugar and water dissolved over medium heat and cooled. (Use to marinate fresh sliced peaches.) Then add a half cup of liquid from the sugar marinated peaches. (Or you could use the brandy marinating jus from your jar of black mission figs instead). Add a squeeze of fresh lemon and a pinch of salt. Add a full cup of ice cubes. Shake vigorously for a half minute.

Pour into stemmed champagne flutes that have been cooled; about three-quarters full. Fill the flute right to the top with my favorite bubbly, sparkling French pink champagne, Royal de Neuville. Park a tiny slice of fresh peach on the rim of the glass. Sip this delicate creation. It's a pink thing!

This is a perfect pairing with a slice of homemade wonderful cream genoise or a slice of fresh peach fruit pastry tart.

Hint: Don't have a cocktail shaker? Use a tightly covered screw-top large glass mason jar.

Any of these recipes using the coquilles as a serving vessel could be switched up using any seafood: Crab, lobster or a seafood mix of your favorites, still using the duxelles and savory sabayon.

For an entrée, you could consider crab cakes, or wonderful two-bite-size cakes made using mixed seafood, sizzling hot, reheated just when ready to serve. They are simply made, even the day before. Offer on a plate with individual seafood savory *crème brûlée*, or an individual seafood panna cotta (set in a shot glass), drizzled with homemade lobster oil. Provide a serving bowl that can be passed at the table, with fresh lemon and lime wedges. And another bowl with mixed lemon lime zest with a tiny serving (espresso) spoon. And yet, another bowl with mixed citrus segments having freshly cut them from between the fruit membranes. (You might add segments of grapefruit if no one is taking certain prescription medicines; some Rx forbid taking with grapefruit of any kind.)

And yet, another table topper: A silver serving bowl of homemade candied citrus rind from your pantry sugar jar. Place a glass bowl inside the silver bowl to keep citrus at bay from direct acidic contact. Diners can choose at will how much of each or all, if they prefer.

You could fill half avocado shells (or hollow out a papaya) with avocado seafood salad on a bed of shredded romaine and iceberg lettuce mix or use mesclun; (spritz the greens with red wine vinegar and extra virgin olive oil 30:70), as part of your entree. For this course, a nice accompaniment is a Canadian Bloody Caesar.

A real "shell-a-bration" of a unique kind. Tell your guests to bring a big appetite and be prepared to indulge over a few hours of at-table enjoyment and be sure to forewarn them dinner is all seafood.

Polenta Mille-Feuille

Holiday entertaining, anyone? Here's a special gourmet plate that has an unspeakable visual quality as well as being a marriage of delicious flavors.

Here's a special gourmet plate that has an unspeakable visual quality as well as being a marriage of delicious flavors.

On occasion when you are holiday entertaining out-of-town guests, or just any visitors any time, think about going the extra mile and prepare this fabulous food as a special welcome. It's not difficult, but perhaps best doable by someone a little experienced in the kitchen and able to multitask.

Make your favorite cheese polenta ahead of time. Let it rest to set firm and measure three equal portions sliced so when assembled they resemble a small pound cake. I prefer slices about 4x6, but you could cut smaller but equal slices such as 2x4.

Each mille-feuille is an individual serving, but a rather large serving. Present with a side serving of crispy bacon rashers and a tiny container (perhaps a glass or crystal salt-cellar) of one of my aioli dipping sauces, along with a few deep-fried whole garlic cloves, for an additional wow factor surprise. (See my recipe below.)

Top a medium thick base slice of the cheese polenta with barely wilted, hot, very well-drained (press the spinach in a colander and put a heavy pot on the spinach for a few minutes) steamed regular spinach, that you have buttered (perhaps use one of your frozen compound herbed butter coins from your freezer log). Be generous. A whole head of spinach only provides a cup of finished product. Again, you can prepare the spinach ahead of time, but don't refrigerate unless absolutely necessary.

I keep containers of my goat cheese spinach grilled sandwich filling in the freezer to use with my omelets, and this would save on time if you thaw and choose to use it in this mille-feuille assembly.

Position another equal measured slice of set polenta on top. Dust with grated mixed wonderful dry cheeses as a bed for fresh very firm, seared on high heat in just a smear of unsalted butter, thick slices of white button mushrooms dusted with thyme, nutmeg and lots of fresh ground pepper. A few grains of salt. Careful. You don't want the mushrooms to weep.

Spoon just a little of my (made earlier) caramelized onions on top of the mushrooms, and top with a matching size third polenta layer.

Top with pre-cooked, then pan-fried in unsalted butter, crushed cooked chestnuts. You can buy beautiful readymade chestnuts in specialty packages, or purchase most top-grade chestnut purée and spread generously. Drizzle with just a tiny bit of noisette. Or deglaze the mushroom sauté pan using Offley Royal Ruby port or Asbach Uralt cognac, and drizzle over the top layer just when ready to serve.

Serve with a long blade sharp steak knife and a long tined fork and a generous size spoon, so not a drop of this delicious treat will be missed.

A rather rustic presentation, it will look its finest served in the center of an oversized dinner plate, perhaps a heavier weight high-grade ceramic plate, warmed with very hot water, rather than on a delicate fine china.

For a full-sized meal, a side serving of medium rare roast duck, venison or lamb could be a nice addition for a very filling dinner meal.

The polenta mille-feuille on its own is a terrific breakfast/brunch. But you might consider topping with two poached runny yolk eggs with freshly made hollandaise, along with a side dish of my grated coarse tomato pulp.

For something attractive for the brunch/breakfast presentation, maybe a grouping of yellow tomato, white tomato, red and green tomato pulp, each in its own little serving dish.

Alternate: If you choose to buy readymade store-bought polenta, it often comes packaged in a large log shape (ideally bought from a high reputation Italian shop). Simply cut large coins perhaps a half-inch-thick and proceed to stack and fill as above and serve, layered, in the round.

You could offer a fabulous seafood version by insetting in the middle layer, chunks of fresh warmed lobster claw meat, or crab or shrimp, drizzled with your melted frozen lobster compound butter coins from your frozen log and/or a drizzle of your homemade lobster oil.

My Aioli Two Ways—Special Aioli Sauce Uses—And A Surprise or Two (Poached and Deep-Fried Garlic, too...)

Use my homemade mayonnaise as a base. Quick and easy to prepare, this mayo will keep in a sterilized screw top glass jar, refrigerated, for six months, so if you live alone or have a small family, there is no need to buy mayonnaise when you can make your own that lasts, with no preservatives of any kind.

In a baked enamel cast-iron pot, measure about a third full of Mazola Corn Oil and heat. Add a dozen individual generous-sized peeled garlic cloves. Increase heat. Poach in the simmering oil until the garlic is mashable; remove the garlic cloves from the oil with a slotted spoon, allow to cool just briefly, and coarsely chop the garlic and add to two cups of mayo. Add herbs or spices if you like, but it's not necessary. This aioli can be used as is, or mash blue cheese into the mix. An amazing sauce with beef, pork, chicken or seafood.

If you have made crab cakes or mixed seafood cakes, a dollop of either sauce on top is wonderful.

Check out my faux blini [insert recipe] and serve with this sauce on a bed of Boston Bibb hydroponically grown lettuce. A little dish of lemon quarters might add to the flavor when squeezed just before indulging.

Serve the cakes on lettuce mounded on a thick slice of my beautiful, Boston brown bread baked in a tin such as a large tomato tin. I used to use coffee tins when coffee was packed in real cans, back in the 1960s. Yes, that's 60 years ago.

Here's another way to use the aioli: Marinate a boneless, skinless chicken breast, or boneless, skinless chicken thighs, in seasoned buttermilk overnight. Seasoning can be paprika, pepper, a sprinkle of thyme and a pinch of nutmeg. I prefer not to salt marinade. Salt the meat when ready to cook.

Pat the chicken dry and dredge the marinated chicken breast in seasoned flour. Deep-fry in the leftover garlic oil pot, at about 350 F. The chicken should cook perfectly in 5–7 minutes, depending on thickness. Salt immediately again when finished deep frying. This is a great, quick way to make dinner when you come home from work, having started the chicken the day before.

Carve the deep-fried chicken breast on the diagonal and drizzle with either aioli and serve on the Boston brown bread or on a grilled brioche, with a handful of fresh watercress.

For a side dish, soak half-inch onion rings in fresh (unused) buttermilk for a couple of hours. Dredge in seasoned semolina flour and deep fry quickly. The onion rings will be cooked when they turn crisp and golden.

You can use the same oil you used for the garlic and the chicken, if you are making onion rings simultaneously. But otherwise, start with fresh oil. At the end of the cooking session, toss the oil. Do not plan to use it another day.

Drain the onion rings on a cookie rack lined with white paper towel. Salt as soon as you remove from the oil. Perhaps sprinkle some of the onion rings with a little cayenne (definitely not if serving to children). Cayenne can actually burn your throat tissue, so if you are not familiar with using it, tread gently at first. It's simply hot peppers.

Drizzle with just a little of the aioli when ready to serve, or use the aioli as a dipping sauce.

You might want to offer either sauce as an accompaniment with sautéed seared or breaded sea scallops. Serve on a bed of shredded mixed lettuce greens. Chop a bit of fresh parsley and/or watercress and add to the aioli.

Or: shred in fine strips on the diagonal, using a very sharp knife, perfectly cooked medium rare prime rib steak, and use the shredded steak to fill a freshly made Yorkshire pudding that you baked using the beef drippings. Deflate and fill the hole with the thinly sliced beef, and serve immediately, topping with a drizzle of the garlic blue cheese aioli.

Now, for those who can never get enough garlic, a special treat.

Having prepared the poached in oil garlic cloves (make as many as you like), immediately when they are barely tender to the point of a sharp knife prick, using a slotted spoon, remove the garlic from the simmering oil pot and place on a white absorbent paper towel on a cake cooling rack.

Quickly whisk together your favorite light batter, even one made with beer. Toss in the whole garlic cloves. Retrieve with a small slotted spoon to let the excess batter drip off, and slide the garlic cloves into 350 F oil in the pot you just poached them in. When the batter is crisp and golden (in just a couple of minutes) remove with the large slotted spoon and place onto a fresh paper towel.

Sprinkle with salt, a few herbs and or spices, and serve at once, alongside any favorite dish. You will find the garlic is medium mild and not at all overpowering. Simply delicious as a nibble treat or with any meat, seafood or poultry dish (a great balance with game), perhaps with a pasta dish, or even as a special salad topper.

Timer and Metric

The particular whole recipe for frangipane otherwise measures liquids in grams. I had never seen such, either, in recipes. However:

Metric isn't metric. Just like English isn't English (easily misunderstood the corroboration of British English, American English, Australian English wherein assumptions made can cause disastrous interpretations). Just one example: Some people say that Canadian (Commonwealth derived) law does not apply in UK. And that Canadian judges' findings hold no weight in British associated cases. And sometimes a given: Lawyers on either side of the ocean cannot interpret one another; yet it's all in English. I digress:

Here in Canada boxes of dry granule laundry soap packages are marked as contents in liters, (meant for liquid measuring), not grams (dry measure), as per what we and our children have been taught. How confusing is this if they ever should live abroad or engage in meaningful work on the continent? Chemistry related job, anyone? Scary.

Off topic, there was a large commercial plane crash in Canada not long after metric measurements became the norm. Apparently, the plane had run out of fuel due to a mistaken confusion brought about by metric conversion when the plane had been fueled for take-off. The plane had run out of fuel and the resultant research and investigation turned up the reason for the crash. What a frightening thought. Sure, hope they don't measure in cl or grams, hoping all fuel-related staff can convert, regardless of what they were taught in school, or training-specific (maybe let the robot do the measuring?)

Overseas mainland (UK doesn't use metric measures in cooking) metric measures are different than Canadian metric indicators. And, of course, Americans don't use metric in cooking in any fashion. Having done boatloads of relocation over the years, this was just one more topic to address if the real estate related relo enjoyed cooking.

In France, a particular recipe calls for 50cl (centiliters) of whole milk, (that would equate to a half liter; why not just say so? Maybe a scientist wrote the recipe.) among other liquids that are referenced in the same recipe as measured in grams.

Others yet, require "dry" butter. So, I set about to discover what is it.

There's something new to be learned constantly.

***

In our Canadian bookstores, we often find cook books that were published in UK, using expressions, measures, and products not available here, although some items can be had in specialty shops. But at least the measurements are not in metric.

Having an insatiable appetite for reading material has provided me supportive education in regard to cooking, especially abroad. I am easily fascinated by these variables.

But mostly recipes are just guidelines, except where chemistry specifics are involved. You are meant to use recipes for ideas mostly, and re-create them to make them your own. But many people don't have time to work out conversions.

Many years ago, I found some valuable tools for my kitchen at a camera supply store, meant for measuring film developer, all with metric and none metric (at least for liquid measures). Tall, plastic-marked containers in the sizes: tiny, small, medium, and large.

Weigh scales are a must for any kitchen, along with a good mortar and pestle. They all too, come in small, medium, and large. Some are more sophisticated than others, reflected in the price, but at any price well worth having.

I practiced in my kitchen till I got it just right, preparing recipes using scales, for developing a few of my own very special Konditorei magnificent dessert recipes.

You can't really make mistakes. Whatever you make can usually be "converted" into something edible. No need to waste.

***

Just as important as timers in your kitchen: thermometers.

You need two thermometers for your oven. Every oven is different; variables include how long an oven takes to get to the set preheat temperature, and that is just one issue. You will find a difference if you are using an electric oven versus a gas fired grill or oven.

When checking for doneness, close the oven door quickly.

No matter the price, make or stove model, oven temperature variables fluctuate, often as much as 25 degrees. There's really no controlling it. The only thing you can do is monitor it, then adjust accordingly by keeping an eye on your oven temperature when using it.

You can help a little to control consistency by not leaving the oven light bulb on, because the light bulb itself gives off heat, not just light.

The back of the oven is always hotter by temperature than the front. And oven racks are adjustable top to bottom for a reason.

Likewise, thermometers fluctuate also, and no guarantee there, either. That's why you need to keep two different makes or models of thermometers in your oven at all times.

Don't hesitate to call for service if you notice that you often have large variables. Your product temperature built in control may have a factory defect issue, even if your appliance is brand new.

By the way, take into consideration your cooking vessels, if you are using glass dishes in baking, for instance, drop your oven temperature 25 degrees, after the oven has reached its preheat setting.

Then for your small tools drawer you will need a candy thermometer for sugar, jams and jellies; and one dedicated to your deep frying; a meat thermometer for kitchen use might break if used in hot sugar, and keep

124

another special thermometer just for grilling, stored within easy access to your BBQ or your grill. And keep them all clean and free of splatters and debris. Clean after each use. Bacteria love to grow in warm gooey places.

A for-kitchen-use-only, keep a stiff firm bristle toothbrush handy and dedicated for use only to clean your timers and thermometers. Most kitchen clean-up brushes are too soft. Rinse well and let the toothbrush thoroughly dry after each use. You will find many uses for a kitchen toothbrush, so dedicate more than one.

If you have enough kitchen or cooking space available, allot a specific storage spot for your thermometers and your timers; perhaps even assign a specific storage container, large enough to spread out the contents, labelled if helpful, in your pantry.

Again, the prices of thermometers vary and it often pays to have duplicates of each. If you search out thermometers online, you will see an abundance of interesting information. But there is no best way or best product regardless of price, but like using timers, using thermometers definitely will help your net result in your gourmet experience.

Here is a sample steak temperature guide preferred by chefs, and by home cooks for keeping control of serving preferences:

120 F–125 F for medium rare, 130 F for medium, and 145 F for well done.

Health scientists recommend not serving meat well-done. Some say char is carcinogenic. And take into consideration that all food continues to cook in its own heat once removed from the cooking heat source.

Tent your cooked food while it rests redistributing its juices. Resting is vital to the process to net a great result.

Tip: When ordering steak at a restaurant, you will see how skilled your waiter and the chef is if you place your order asking for a temperature preference rather than placing your order as: Medium rare or medium well, for example.

It will be an indicator to the kitchen that you take food preparation seriously. Their definitions as to doneness might not match yours, but a specific temperature guide is exactly that.

Your wait-staff reaction will speak volumes. But surely the chef will understand. If you are told they don't use thermometers, or you see raised eyebrows or rolled back eyeballs, you might consider not to book a return engagement.

Note: One of the chief complaints about wedding food if serving plated is that it is either cold when the food is meant to be hot, or it's too well-done, over cooked. Hot food should be served on a hot serving plate, definitely not on a cold plate. But many things have to be taken into consideration in the prep kitchen.

***

Using your smart phone in the kitchen—speaking of being organized.

Timer, Timer, Timer—get more than one…and then there's your grill pan.

Stop the madness. No fuss. No mess. No waste. Do not overcook things ever again.

One of the most important tools in your kitchen is your timer. It is your friend. Using your timer wisely and listening to it, and reacting accordingly, will help you produce wonderful tender, melt in your mouth food. Your timer is as important as your ingredients.

Most stoves have a timer, or at least a clock. If you don't have a timer, watch your clock carefully. If you have a smart phone, set the timer on the phone. Most people have so much on their minds these days, they rely heavily on technology. Such a simple thing, to be a helper in the kitchen, is the timer on the smart phone. We all multitask. But your food in the cooking process does not take that into consideration. It demands your full attention, and if you are one whose mind gets distracted easily, for sure you will find using a timer helpful.

But set the sound loud enough so you can't miss it. Even if you have a timer, you will find you need more than one. And you will learn to listen to its alert.

If you are cooking a thick steak or pork chop, set the timer for 4 minutes initially while the grill marks happen on the meat, using high heat. If you need 5 minutes, that extra minute will happen while you reach for your tongs. Use tongs, never a fork when working with meat. You don't want to pierce the meat, or you will lose those most important and delicious, juices.

At 4 minutes, turn the meat. You will have started the cooking process on high heat, to sear the surface of the meat, get those beautiful grill marks, and seal in the juices. As you turn the meat, turn down the heat to minimum, or lift the grill pan off the burner. The cast iron grill pan will retain its high heat for several minutes longer.

If you are using the BBQ, set one part for high heat and the other at low or medium. Using an oiled clean cloth, (and tongs) oil the grill veins. Set the timer for 3 minutes, and grill the meat to get great grill marks, then turn and move the meat to the less hot portion for another three minutes. Check with a sharp knife to check for doneness. Do not overcook.

Back to the stovetop burner method: To complete the task, chefs often get their grill marks on, and then use the oven to complete the cooking process. At home, cooks often complete the cooking process on the stovetop, especially in hot weather when they don't want to heat up the kitchen excessively, preheating their oven.

Don't forget; when cooking is complete, let the meat rest for at least 5 to 10 minutes, so the internal juices redistribute. Tent with tinfoil. You won't have wasted juices on the plate. Carve on the diagonal, thick or thin, as your preference dictates. You will have the best meat plate if you follow these simple instructions.

And, use your timer. Right away you will notice a difference in your cooking results. I repeat. Your timer is your friend. Your smart phone is a great accessory in your kitchen.

Smartphone—Here's a useful and important smartphone tip: If you don't wear your smart phone as a body appendage, you will park your phone in many places when not in use.

Most users have a cover hand back wrap on their phones, leaving the screen open and accessible. When you "park" your phone on a bathroom counter or elsewhere, turn it open screen face side down. This provides a little extra protection from splashes or for example a hair brush or other in use bathroom item that might fall onto the screen and break it.

Steam in excess in a slower or while running a hot bath is not a good environment for your phone. But it's sometimes necessary to keep the phone handy if expecting an important call; so, package wrap your phone in a clean dry facecloth and put it in a safe spot where you won't accidentally grab the facecloth forgetting your phone is in it. Maybe even put the wrapped phone in the drawer or cupboard. The idea is to keep the smart phone away from the moisture. I shared this idea with an Apple rep during a conversation and she said she would pass it on.

Easy Clean Grill Pan

And then there's the stovetop grill pan cleanup, with ribs, or veins: how do you clean yours? I can't bear to see some of the grill pans people cook on. No, you don't want to wash the grill pan with cleaning materials that leave a (soapy) residue on the cast iron. It's perfectly okay to clean the bottom of the pan using a granular cleaner (rinse well), the part that comes in contact with the stove top burner; you need to keep the bottom spotless, too, to get the best use from the grill pan when cooking. Use a granular cleaner such as Comet powder, but definitely not for the inside of the grill pan. Picture this: You cook your steak or pork chop and the juice residue is stuck like glue, and will get more so if left too long without cleaning.

But let's go back to the beginning. You start with a wonderful, fresh grill pan. Pour a little of your favorite cooking oil on the hot grill pan. Careful, 'cause it's *hot*. Using a clean throw away cloth, or a wad of paper towel, saturated in oil, rub over the grill veins. Now you have a perfect surface on which to cook.

When you are finished cooking, boil a little water and deglaze, yes, deglaze the grill pan right away. And save those wonderful drippings. Pour the drippings into a waiting wide mouth bowl.

Put a clean washing dishcloth in the bottom of your sink. Using an edible but cheaper oil, perhaps a cup of oil, (for me, I don't cook with Canola, but I keep a bottle of it handy, expressly for this use) pour the oil into the grill pan, in the sink. Let it sit overnight or for at least a couple of hours.

Boil water and dilute the oil in the grill pan and dispose in a trash-able container. Next, sprinkle the grill pan with a half cup of plain ordinary baking soda, and a cup of plain white vinegar. Watch the bubbles. Just like chemistry class.

Instant, like new. Just look at your grill pan. Again, using boiling hot water or your tap at its highest heat, rinse the grill pan completely. Wipe the excess water away using a toss-away or paper towel. Turn on the stovetop burner till it is really hot. Turn it off. Place the grill pan on the turned off hot burner just briefly, to get rid of any excess water.

Move the grill pan to another burner that has not recently been hot. Any water residue will evaporate and you're ready to grill, again. Keep all your utensils sparkling clean the safe and easy way. This alone will improve all your results, especially if you use a timer.

And, there are 9 million Canadian expats living throughout other parts of the world; not all are government employees.

This collection of recipes is from all my own originals, some from as far back as the 1970s, developed in my own kitchen, beginning when I was in my mid-30s, as newspaper gourmet cooking columns of the day, known as "Gourmet Cooking with Carolyne," and others in the collection as my own copyrighted columns at Canada's leading real estate news magazine, REM.

I have included a foreword that speaks a little to how I became a food writer and recipe developer. I was never interested in sports. I had a voracious appetite for reading.

Having been brought up as an only child, surrounded only by adults, I became a childhood armchair traveler indulging in walls of National Geographic magazines, the weekend Star-Weekly newspaper magazine, Family Circle and Woman's Day magazines, along with my own personal set of Colliers Encyclopedia. Television didn't become available at large, until the early 1950s, and hardly anyone had one. Once available, there was only one channel available for years. But radios were still very much in vogue, and you had to have an annual license to be allowed to listen to your own radio in your own house.

There was nothing in either National Geo or Colliers about cooking as such. But there was plenty about cultures and diversification, and diaspora. Accompanied by our education curriculum including geography and history classes, I would expand my learning by looking up extended materials, much like students have Google at their beck and call today.

In what for years had been called Domestic Science classes, in the 1940s became known as Home Economics classes, introduced to students round about Grade 7 in many school curricula.

I recently read an out of print reprint of an old scholarly academic interpretation of the times, titled: "Perfection Salad," nothing to do with Salad per se, and a good example of how a book title can be very misleading.